The Journey

God's Call & Provision For Us To Begin & Complete Our Return To Him

Volume 2 of "The Highest Calling of All Series"

by Larry Trammell

Ablaze Productions!, Inc.
P.O. Box 956236
Duluth, GA (USA)   30095-9504
770.476.0230, ext. 2
www.ablazeministries.com

Assistance with desktop publishing & cover art by:
Higher Ground Studios, Inc.
www.highergroundstudios.com

The Journey

God's Call & Provision For Us To Begin & Complete Our Return To Him

Teacher & Student Workbook Editions Are Available

Volume 2 [ISBN 0-9624370-2-6] *of*
"The Highest Calling Of All" Series
[complete series consists of 14 Volumes; ISBN 0-9714637-0-0]

Library of Congress Card Number: 2001118888

Copyright © 1996 by *Larry Trammell*
New Edition: 2003

Desktop Publishing & Cover Art: Ablaze Productions!, Inc.
Box 956236/ Duluth, GA (USA)/ 30095-9504 770.476.0230, ext. 2/
www.ablazeministries.com &
Higher Ground Studios, Inc./ Lawrenceville, GA   770.963.1901/
www.highergroundstudios.com

—Important Note From the Author Regarding Bible Versions Referenced—

Various versions of the Bible are utilized in this book. For the sake of clarity, I often combine different translations when quoting from Scripture. "Hybrid" quotes are thus sometimes rendered. While not altering the meaning, such quotations read slightly differently from the translations utilized. References to the Godhead are capitalized, even when a version of the Bible to which I am referring does not. Also, from time to time I italicize various words that I desire the reader to emphasize.

Rather than repeatedly listing the different versions referenced or having "based on" and "from" this or that version scattered throughout this work, Bible versions used are listed below, thereby giving credit where it is due and complying with copyright law. Hopefully, reading will be less broken and disjointed without these credits being listed in the text.

The Authorized (King James) Version.
I thank God for William Tyndale and others like him who lay down their lives
for the preservation and propagation of the Truth of The Bible—*the* Scriptures of God.

The Amplified Bible. Old Testament copyright © 1965, 1987
by The Zondervan Corporation. The Amplified New Testament copyright 1958, 1987
The Lockman Foundation. Used by permission.

The New King James Version. Copyright © 1979, 1980, 1982,
Thomas Nelson Inc., Publishers.

The New International Version. Copyright © 1973, 1978, 1984
International Bible Society. Used by permission of Zondervan Bible Publishers.

The New American Standard Bible, © 1960, 1962, 1963, 1968, 1971, 1972, 1973, 1975, 1977
by The Lockman Foundation. Used by permission.

The New Century Version of the Bible, copyright © 1987, 1988, 1991
by Word Publishing, Dallas, Texas 75234. Used by permission.

The Holy Bible, Contemporary English Version, copyright © 1995.
Used by permission.

The Living Bible, copyright © 1971.
Used by permission of Tyndale House Publishers, Inc., Wheaton, Illinois 60189. All rights reserved.

Also, I am so very thankful for **Strong's Exhaustive Concordance of the Bible,**
published by Riverside Book and Bible House.
It's such a wonderful blessing, and I have referred to it very often.

Acknowledgments

Chris Strong: A friend and man of God who helped me begin and persevere in The Journey. He has "eternal perspective" and "sees" The Kingdom.

Jan and Vince Ghioto: They were like spiritual parents, giving me much love, exhortation, and food (spiritual *and* physical), especially in my teen years.

John and Lee Rosser: Precious friends who have helped us as well as so many others to either begin *The Journey* or be strengthened in our temporary sojourn. Their reward will be great for establishing and helping so many on the road that leads to life. Blessings be upon them!

Gary and Teresa Patterson: Their love, their zealous, panting love for God, their godliness, wise counsel, and sound example of discipleship to Jesus Christ have helped me maintain my footing on *The Journey.*

Larry Reese: For allowing me the honor and pure joy of teaching in the Raffa Frontline Ministries' School of Discipleship, and for his willingness for me to follow the Spirit of God. He loves God and hears His voice.

Shirley Gregory: For bestowing on me the honor and pure joy of teaching in the Joshua School of Ministries, and for her willingness for me to follow the Spirit of God without restraint. She is a mother in Israel, full of love for Jesus, grace, worship, hunger, and truth.

Stephanie Ray Johnson: "My dear sister," for this book's beautiful cover, her computer skills, love, friendship, and prayers. Because of her, many projects have been able to be completed.

Cliff and Stacy: My wonderful and precious children. How I love them! They bring such joy and honor to the Lord Jesus Christ and their family. I honor them for becoming mature messengers of Christ— vessels in and through whom He has His way, leading others by following Him and serving them. They are precious, pursuing pilgrims on *The Journey.*

Alice: My bride. My pride, my joy, my crown, and my choice on whom I have set my love. Many daughters have done nobly, but *she excels them all!* [Based on Proverbs 31:29.] She is my partner and help meet on *The Journey.*

***Much* proofreading and/or editorial input:** Barbie Eslin, Kim Ramos, Mary Roberts, Stacy Walker, Alice Trammell, and Judy Hess.

Those of you I did not mention here are, nonetheless, mentioned in Heaven. None of your labors of love will be unrewarded. Jesus is faithful, and, as you have done it to one of the least of His people, you have done it to Him.

Therefore, He and I both thank you (and bless you, too)!

All the saints who love us and allow us to love them

Our family and fellow sojourners. *Remember:* We're pilgrims just passing through, so maintain an Eternal Perspective with your hearts and minds set on unseen things that are above, where Christ is. He is our Inheritance and soon to return Bridegroom. May He find us awake, prepared, and eagerly awaiting Him, eagerly persisting on *The Journey.*

Dedication & Exhortation

To all who recognize their need to begin
the journey back home to the heart of
the Heavenly Father.

Hear His warnings and answer His call.

He loves you enough to choose you, call you,
change you, and never forsake you
so that you and He can enjoy intimate fellowship
together...forever.

May your journey begin and never end until,
by His grace, you are in His arms
and gazing into His face
in His eternal kingdom.

Turn from all else, say "Yes!" to Him,
and follow Him wholeheartedly—
By His mercy and grace,
you can both begin and complete
The Journey.

Volume 2 of "The Highest Calling Of All" series

The Journey
God's Call & Provision For Us To Begin & Complete Our Return To Him

TABLE OF CONTENTS

Introduction
(Don't Skip This!)

*I*n this second volume of "The Highest Calling Of All" Series, we discuss beginnings and endings—beginnings such as the origins of Satan, his rebellion of sin, the origin of pain and death, the beginning of man and his deadly demise, and God's marvelous and thorough response and answer that ends all the dilemmas of His wounded creation.

You may feel that many things discussed in this book are rudimentary and already very familiar to you. Even if this is true, I strongly encourage you to read these contents prayerfully, anyway. After all, even things usually thought of as "basic" are foundational, vital, and necessary components of our lives if we desire to really know the Lord and grow to full stature in Him—only when a solid foundation has been laid can we build a sure and steadfast life on it.

Also, perhaps you will find that a part of your foundation is lacking or in need of strengthening. Hopefully, these contents will be used by God's Holy Spirit to help "shore it up" so that the character of Jesus can be seen without taint in you.

So, before we discuss so-called "deeper" things regarding the Ever Living God and His kingdom, before we can have meaningful and ever deepening fellowship with Him, we should be certain that we are His children, citizens of His eternal kingdom. First relationship, then fellowship—genuine relationship with God must first be established before intimate fellowship with Him can occur.

Liar And/Or Lunatic Or Lord?

In The Revelation 1:8 and 11; 21:6; and 22:13, Jesus declared Himself to be "the Alpha and Omega—the Beginning and the End." If we allow this truth to really sink in and become a part of us, we come to the realization that we start our journey on the path of spiritual life at our destination. That is, we start with Jesus and end with Jesus: It is all centered on JESUS!!! *He* is to be our focus and pursuit. Colossians 3:4 even declares Him to be our very life.

He will not let us merely accept Him as a prophet, for no genuine, faithful prophet would ever accept worship and claim to actually be God as He did in John 8:58. There we read that He proclaimed Himself to be "I Am"—the most sacred name for God among Jews.

Neither will He allow us to relegate Him to a place among many so-called "gods," for in John 14:6, He declared Himself to be *The* Way, *The* Truth, and *The* Life, as well as the *only* means whereby we can have right standing with God and sweet fellowship with Him.

According to His claims, we cannot rightfully consider Him to be merely a teacher, a prophet, one of many so-called "gods," or even just a good person (after all, such a person would not claim to be something that he is not). Jesus is either a liar and/or a lunatic or the Son of God and the Lord as He claimed.

I do not hesitate to declare boldly that He is Who He and His apostles claimed Him to be. Not only have I experienced His reality, but the transformed lives of those who truly love and follow Him attest to His validity.

If you have not personally experienced this transformation, I urge you at the very least to be open to Him and His revealing of Himself to you. Talk to Him as you would another person, for that is what He is—the Person from Whom all "Personhood" derives its name.

To those of us who are already re-created spiritually by God's Spirit, let's seriously examine ourselves and make our "calling and election certain and sure." [2 Peter 1:10.] Although the process is sometimes extremely painful, difficult, and requires that we greatly humble ourselves, He Who is the incomparable Reward is more than worth it. However, know of a certainty that the ability to love and obey the Lord (or even having desires to do so) are not part of our "human" nature. We desperately need God. He—not us—is the source of *all* righteousness. Any desire for goodness or any ability to truly do what is right in His sight must come from Him. We must not try to fulfill the will of God without God. Know that such independent pride is doomed to failure, not only because of our own innate inadequacies, but because the Lord Himself will severely resist such a self-reliant attitude.

So, look away from all distractions to Jesus and, by His direction and with His help, stir up what He has already placed in you by His Holy Spirit. By God's mercy and grace, let us complete *The Journey* of journeys back into Papa's arms...

The Holy Bible reveals that God is holy, just, good, sovereignly reigning over all, and the Author of love, wisdom, joy, beauty, peace, and life. Why, then, is His creation full of lust, injustice, wickedness, hatred, chaos, sadness, confusion, fear, evil, and the spectre of death? How did we get into this predicament? What's the purpose of existence? Will the cycle of life and death, good and evil, be perpetuated forever? Is there a lasting satisfaction available to the seeking, hungry soul? What, if anything, can be done to remedy the tragic dichotomies of life?

There are answers to these tough questions, and—thank God!—*He* has done what was needed, providing a remedy for humanity's rebellious, costliest folly…

—1—

The End Of The Beginning

Before anything else existed, there was God—the only One with no beginning: eternal, unchangeable, all powerful, all knowing, holy, and whole—complete in and of Himself. Everything that exists, things visible and invisible—the *all*—was contained in Him and emanated from Him at His command. He created everything out of nothing but Himself, and it His by the power of this one and only God that it is sustained.

Beyond our finite minds to fully conceive, the identity and the revelation of this infinite, spirit Being are comprised of three distinct Persons Who are one in essence and Who have revealed Themselves to us as The Father, The Son, And The Holy Spirit. This almighty God could have remained eternally content with the fellowship He enjoyed within His tri-existence, but He chose to reveal Himself to a creation that He loves intensely. In particular, He desired to reveal Himself to, in and through a willing humanity who would have the choice to be a part of what could be called "a celestial family," with this wonderful, loving God at the head—loving all and sustaining all.

Existing beyond the limitations of His creation, He is known only as He allows Himself to be known. In other words, no one hungers for God or "finds" God on their own. Instead, He calls to the human heart and then reveals Himself to responsive, seeking souls. For He endowed humanity with the ability to choose whether to yearn for Him or turn from Him.

But let's not get ahead of ourselves...

In the beginning, before His creation of mankind, God's masterful work of creation was perfect—untainted and full of wonder, delight, and His own character, marked most distinctly by what we know as "love." [How wonderful it is that the Creator and Sustainer of all is One Who's very being and essence defines benevolence.]

A vast number of powerful spirit beings known as angels were created by God to worship Him, serve Him, and bring delight. In their faithfulness to Him, they found personal fulfillment in their faithfulness to Him. Among these creatures, none was honored with as exalted a position as Lucifer—a mighty angel of the Cherub order. [Two of the main texts where we can discover more about him are Isaiah 14:12-20 and Ezekiel 28:11-19.] He was resplendent in the beauty and glory of His Creator (his name even means "shining one," "light bringer," or "bearer of light"). More than likely, he was the leader of the hosts of creation in the worship of the Deity.

Lucifer's Fatal, Flawed Folly And Fall

However, leading worship to God was not enough for him. Perhaps, one day, as the teeming, angelic hosts gave praise and worship to God, Lucifer imagined what it would be like to have them sing *his* praises, not God's. Iniquity—the willful refusal to embrace that which is godly and right—was conceived in Lucifer when he gave birth to selfishness; conceived when he chose to be preoccupied with himself instead of remaining focused on God. Rather than gratefully recognize and thankfully acknowledge that it was God Who gave him everything he had and made him everything he was, his becoming enamored and preoccupied with himself twisted and perverted his thinking, leading him to think along these lines of insane, self-destructive, and murderous egomania:

*Look at **ME**—THE ULTIMATE AND UNIQUE ONE; soooo beautiful—too beautiful to be less than the center of attention. I'M not just the light bearer—I am THE LIGHT!*

*All will gaze at ME and be amazed, for **I** am THE ONE who will lead all of creation in the casting off of the shackles of devotion to the creator and of focus on him. I will sit at the helm of glorious self-discovery. I will be gazed upon and admired—yes, even worshiped. As all creatures take their eyes off of **him**, they will embark on the path of self-fulfillment, which will ultimately lead them to **ME** (glorious **ME**) ruling and reigning the chaos and confusion that shall ensue. For I shall head-up the insubordination of these stupid, insipid creatures against their creator—this one who would chain everything everywhere with his boring, self-denying will. But I will not deny MY desires for his will again. Instead, all creation will bend to **ME** and **MY** indomitable will. I will set creation free so that all will be subordinate to ME. I will lead all creatures to satisfy themselves and, as they do, they shall be inexorably drawn into my fierce embrace of darkness and death. I will be able to do this because I am THE INVINCIBLE GREAT, DARK LORD OF LIGHT—LUCIFER, THE SHINING LORD OF DARKNESS; the ONE to be feared; THE **I AM!** And soon, I will forever hold the scepter of Heaven in MY beautiful, ruthless hands. Then ALL—including the hated hosts of Heaven with its despicable despot—will come and grovel at MY feet.*

*Convincing them that they shall be their own masters, in reality they will be MY pawns and puppets in MY brilliant plan to dominate everything everywhere with MYSELF. As I get everyone to focus on and supposedly live for themselves, they shall actually be offering their worthless, stupid lives to ME—THE LORD OF SELF AND SELFISHNESS! Cut off from their creator, **I** will re-create all creatures in **MY** image—I WHO loved MYSELF instead of **him**(!); I WHO became...I WHO was, and is, and shall forever be GOD!!! All of creation will be inverted the way it should be—right will become wrong and wrong right, light will become darkness and darkness light—and I will be like "the most high."*

But, I will not tolerate a rival. So, being like him, I shall then destroy him and his mangy minions, claim MY rightful title, ascend the throne—MY throne—and take MY place at the head of creation. Forever I, THE GLORIOUS ONE, will be feared, honored, adored, and worshipped as GOD MOST HIGH!

Thus, MY foe—the "most heinous"—shall be given a permanent hiatus.

So, sin and its insanity was born and fueled in the warped heart and twisted mind of Lucifer to the extent that he—one who was created—thought he could subvert and conquer the Creator.

Insane folly indeed.

However, having chosen to take his focus off of God and place it on himself, he unwittingly sealed his damnation and fiery fate. Self-absorption produced its sure fruit—self-destruction, for the Creator had placed within all of His creatures the need to focus on the Godhead and fellowship with Them. But Lucifer chose to have no more of that. His selfishness gripped him relentlessly and completely. Driven and consumed by his own tormenting thoughts, he became flooded with anarchy, illusions of grandeur, self-aggrandizement, and a macabre fascination with perversion and death. His pride produced an insatiable lust for pleasure and power that would eventually infect the creation like a destructive, terminal virus, and lust proved to be the means by which the stamp of Lucifer's nature is placed on all that is of this present world. We read of this in 2 Peter 1:4. It reveals that the corruption that is in the world is here through lust—the world that 1 John 5:19 tells us "lies in the lap or the power of the evil one." This corruption that is in the world was first spawned in the heart, mind, and soul of the lustful, self-corrupted Lucifer.

Thus, he maligned, marred, abused, distorted, and corrupted his heavenly, shining visage and all of the great beauty and brilliance bestowed on him by his benevolent Creator. Although he would often present himself throughout the following centuries as an angel of light, such would be a lying ruse to hide the reality of his true nature—one of deceptive darkness, desperation, despondency, destruction, and diabolical despising of all that is of God. Because of this, the anchorless and perverted Lucifer became the first and father of all that vomits forth filth and dispenses death. Moral and spiritual garbage overflowed from his hardened heart that had intentionally renounced and turned in hatred from all light and holiness—qualities that he now despised because they so ebulliently flowed from the Creator. Because of this willful rejection of God Who is light, Lucifer's inner being was forever plunged into total darkness. How far he had fallen!

He exchanged the benevolence of his Creator for unabated rebellion. This in turn quickly flooded him with malevolence and all of its attending loneliness, grief, sadness, pain, darkness, and death. His gifted mind became so thoroughly polluted and warped that he was driven to sociopathic, homicidal insanity. The love he originally had for the Lord was replaced with a vehement hatred towards Him so great that Lucifer would stop at nothing in his attempts to cause the Lord to feel even the slightest amount of sadness and pain.

So, he who more than likely had been given a primary role in leading others in reverent, joyful worship to God became the inglorious leader and spiritual father of every angel and human who would ever rebel against the Lord God. Hence, all who have ever disdained the Lord by despising His authority have aligned themselves with Lucifer—the author of rebellious self-centeredness.

Pride reached its putrid pinnacle when Lucifer—so full of himself and now and forever totally blind and resistant to the Truth—became filled with such delusion that he actually chose to mount a revolt against God. Lucifer's foiled attempt produced damning, disastrous results.

The Fight

Having become void of all light and truth, Lucifer was filled instead with deep darkness and deception. In him was fulfilled the axiom that "he who rejects truth is deceived and becomes a deceiver, for the deceived deceive." And so Lucifer The Most Deceived became also Lucifer The Father Of All Lies And Liars; the one in whom there is no more light or truth. With beguiling craftiness and lofty sounding yet deceptive intrigue, he actually persuaded a minority of the angelic hosts (though they still were significant in number) to follow him in his maniacal anarchy and rebellion against God and His authority. So, Lucifer and his renegade legions, filled with spiritual darkness and death, set out to attempt to overthrow God—the Source of true, genuine light and life.

As Lucifer fostered, nurtured, and spread a desire to usurp the glory and authority that rightfully belonged to God alone, sin and its discord flowed from his darkened psyche and seared conscience, marring the transcendent unity and perfection of creation. Soon, water, earth, and air would become polluted, the life of created things would ebb and then cease in the bony grip of death, and much of music—a chief treasure of Heaven full of perfect beauty and uplifting melody and harmony intended by God to honor Him, bring His joy, and reveal aspects of His ways and nature—would be used to spread chaos, depravity, and moral darkness. Its lofty purpose would become tainted and torn with discordant, dissonant sounds that spewed from the hardened heart of the enemy.

But before flooding the earth with his filth, Lucifer first spewed his venom in the very courts of Heaven in his bid for the throne of God. Fires of the Luciferic rebellion exploded with vehement force and fury, driven by Lucifer's self-absorption. Thus, there was a terrible fight in the heavens. But Satan's disruption of the haven of Heaven's courts was short-lived, for he and his armies were no match for the Almighty. Although such knowledge seems obvious, in his insanity, Lucifer the creature forgot that he was just exactly that—a *creature,* not God the Creator. He was a cherub created to worship (as we were all created to do), but he was never to be worshiped. So, God cast the devil from His Presence and out of the courts of Heaven along with his rebellious, disruptive and deceived angelic followers.

Rather than being exalted and able to claim the title "King of Creation," Lucifer was condemned and became known as "the lord of the flies," "the prince of darkness," "the devil," "Satan—the adversary," and many other contemptible names and titles. As previously mentioned, he still deceptively transforms himself into an angel of light in his unrelenting efforts to deceive all of creation. However, in reality, he is full of total, utter darkness, and ultimately offers nothing but destruction, eternal misery, and woe.

The Test—The Tool

Nonetheless, in His wisdom, God chose to turn what Satan meant for evil into a tool to help establish and develop that which is pure, righteous, and good (how this frustrates Satan!). He decided to use the devil's rebellion as a means of:

1) displaying (according to Ephesians 3:10) the many sided wisdom of God to angelic beings who would learn of His ways by observing how God would relate to those who would call upon Him and continue to grow in their love for Him; and

2) testing and perfecting a people who would be given the choice of whether they would know, love, and obey God.

Those who would choose Him and His ways, willingly submitting themselves to Him, would be allowed to reign with Him forever. On the other hand, those who spurned His incalculable offer to follow Him—choosing instead to walk in the rebellious and self-centered footsteps of Lucifer—would suffer the same, ultimate end as he. This would be eternal damnation in a place of self-imposed humiliation, destruction, and suffering, cutoff from God and the hope of reprieve.

Therefore, in order to set up "the test," God allowed Satan and his hordes to have access to "Earth." After all, Satan had become the archenemy of God and of all that God holds dear. Ever since then, he has vehemently hated all people, most especially those who respond in willing submission to God and His loving, merciful forgiveness and sin-conquering grace. God's children/disciples have always been the objects of much of God's most tender affections and loftiest plans. They were even chosen by God to be vessels that would eternally display the manifest glory of God revealed to them and in them. Because of this, the hate-filled, insanely jealous Satan set his murderous intents on the destruction of God's plan for them.

The End Of The Beginning had come, but it wasn't yet the beginning of the end.

Not yet...

2

Our Demise And Deadly "Disease"

*T*he home of the very first humans—Adam and Eve—was a place called "Eden." Within Eden was a garden of indescribable beauty. Adam and Eve cared for Eden's garden and one another with joy and had blissful fellowship with God.

Life was beautiful. Joyful. Peaceful. There was no fear, lustful selfishness, or worry. Unmarred by sin, pain, or death, humanity's home was full of the perfect glory of its perfect Creator. In Genesis, chapter two, however, we begin to discover how this paradise of pristine beauty and perfection became spoiled and infected with sin and death...

Continuing in Genesis 3, we read of a conversation that Eve had with a gorgeous, talking serpent. Before discounting this as pure fancy, recall that this occurred during a time when the earth was in a perfect state and condition. Because sin, (with its resultant deterioration and death) has been released into the earth, things were quite different then than they are now.

So, perhaps Adam and Eve had an ability to converse with animals. The text does seem to indicate that Eve was quite comfortable talking with him, possibly indicating that she had talked with this and/or other animals in days gone by. Either way, this time the serpent was housing within him the leader of the angelic revolt in Heaven, the cunning and fallen cherub—Lucifer the liar. As a spirit being, Lucifer could inhabit some physical things, and, this time, he chose to inhabit a willing snake.

The Lie

Dressed in his finest "serpent suit," he masked his diabolical intentions, probably approaching Eve in a seemingly warm, non-threatening way. Through the mouth of the snake, He spoke his deadly deceptions to her with words to this effect...

"Don't worry about what God has told you—forget about it. You'll be like God if you just do as *I* say and do your own thing. You'll be your own person, free of His control and intervention. You gotta look out for 'Number 1!' You don't need God. You can live independently of Him."

What a lie—*the* lie, as a matter of fact.

God had allowed Adam and Eve to partake of every fruit-bearing tree in the garden except one. In Genesis 2:16-17, we read: "And the Lord God commanded the man, 'You are free to eat from any tree in the garden; but you must not eat from the tree of the knowledge of good and evil...'" To partake of this tree would mean that Adam would be:

1) embracing everything that is opposed to a life of humble dependency on God and obedience to Him, and

2) choosing to turn from a life of selfless dependency on God to a life of selfish self-sufficiency.

The Lord wanted humanity to look to Him for wisdom, not to an innate knowledge born of living independently of Him. He desired that they would choose to forever live their lives in total, trusting, and joyful dependency on Him that is born of relationship with Him. He wanted them to come to really know Him as He personally taught them His ways and character, bringing them into greater and greater union with Him and conformity to His very own nature. His desire was for them to experience the true purpose and fullness of life that can come only through ever-deepening friendship and fellowship with Him. But He would not do this without their permission.

He did not want them to be mere robots with programmed responses. Instead, He wanted relationship and fellowship with them that flowed from their own willingness, desire, and choice to know Him, love Him, and obey Him. For this reason, He created them with what we now call "free will." This enabled them to determine their destinies by either freely choosing to love Him and His ways or by choosing to turn from Him.

For, though Adam and Eve were perfect when they were created (in the sense that the bondages, limitations, and moral weaknesses of sin were not working within them), they were also perfectly innocent, and God had something more in mind when He created them than that they simply remain innocent. He wanted them to grow and develop spiritually, developing godly character, and the only way to develop such righteous character is for innocence to be morally tested. Whenever innocence faces and overcomes temptations to choose sin over righteousness, the result is proven, mature, godly character. Without the option to make a wrong choice and go our own way, we would never fully appreciate and even most deeply love God's choices and ways. Therefore, God gave Adam and Eve (and every one who came after them) the wonderful yet potentially damning power of personal choice, placing within them that spiritual and moral compass we call "conscience" to righteously guide and influence their free will.

Unfortunately, they stubbornly and tragically disobeyed Him, partaking of the fruit of the forbidden tree. In doing so, they polluted their consciences. They chose to embrace "the lie" (consisting of falsely believing that any creature can flourish or even survive without living in total reliance on the Creator and obedience to Him). Embracing "the lie" causes us to seek to discover ultimate and fulfilling purpose in life apart from total dependency on God and an ever-deepening relationship with Him.

The Plunge Into Lucifer's Rebellious Cesspool

By embracing the lie, Adam and Eve embraced the liar—Satan (the one Jesus called "the father of lies" in John 8:44). Their decision to turn from God's commandment put them and their descendants—all of humanity—in league with Satan and under his tyrannical rule and domination. By choosing to follow him in his foolish folly of defying God, they became part of "The Rebellion" of sin the devil began in Heaven against Him.

At the heart of Satan's rebellion is a refusal to acknowledge God as God and worship Him with a thankful heart. It exalts the will of the creature over the will of the Creator. It is self-seeking instead of God-seeking. And it always leads to destruction, chaos, and death because it rejects the Living God—He Who is the only source of wholeness, order, and life. It loves to talk *about* God without submitting *to* God—allowing Him the right to rule and reign. Wanting God only on its own terms (not His), it accepts fables over facts and religious interpretation over God's Spirit's revelation.

Form over freedom.

Ritual over reality.

Religion *about* God instead of relationship *with* Him.

Whether consciously or not, all of us have willfully turned from the Lord, thinking that we are doing "our own thing." However, this, too, is a lie in and of itself, for we are not really doing *our own* thing. We are, in actuality, embracing the rebellious nature of Lucifer and participating in His rebellious "thing." Whenever we embrace Satan's lying temptations, we grant him authority in our lives, just as Adam and Eve did.

Even in the lives of God's children, following the tempter gives him a right of access into areas of their lives that would normally be off limits to him due to the victory that Christ secured on their behalf. In other words, embracing temptations is to embrace the tempter. Thank God, Satan's authority and right of access in our lives can be removed, but only through sincere, godly repentance. Repentance involves us not only acknowledging our errors and willful disobedience of God and His ways. It also entails us rejecting Satan and his lies by turning from them to do the will of the Lord. True repentance produces a turning *from* Satan *and* a turning *to* God.

The Essence Of Sin And Sins. Independence Is Sindependence

Living independently of the Lord is actually anarchy and rebellion against Him and is the essence of sin—to be independent is to be *sin*dependent. This inward, unseen condition of rebellion against God called "sin" that is in the hearts and minds of people produces outward, visible actions and manifestations called "sins." Sin is the root, and sins are its fruit.

If we thought we would destroy a tree by cutting off its branches or its fruit, we would be greatly mistaken. Trimming a tree back will not destroy the tree. Instead, such pruning actually causes it to produce even more fruit.

In a similar way, when we attempt to "clean up our act"—purifying our actions and attitudes—in our own strength, we merely harden our hearts toward God and ensure that we will continue in rebellion against Him, even if some of our outward displays of anarchy are curbed. The reason for this is that just as a tree or plant must be destroyed from its roots if we do not want it to ever bear fruit again, we must destroy the root of sin in our lives if we desire to be free from the evidences of sin—the *sins* that are the "fruit" of *sin*.

In other words, if wrong thinking and wrongdoing are to be removed from us, we must deal with the root of wickedness in our hearts. This is what produces the spiritually fatal attempt to live rebelliously independent of God and fills us with prideful self-sufficiency. Only if the root of living independently of God is destroyed will the fruit of living wasted lives full of evil also be destroyed—*sin* must be destroyed if we desire to see *sins* destroyed.

In place of the deadly fruit of sin, the life giving fruit of God's Spirit (which are the character traits of His Son, listed in Galatians 5:22-23) must be cultivated and allowed to grow in our lives. They are love, joy, peace, patience, kindness, goodness, faithfulness, gentleness, and self-control. These evidences of God's life in us—the result of having received salvation—can occur only as we live in obedience to God by relying totally on the enabling power of His Holy Spirit.

The Fall And Its Consequences

Scripture speaks of the total, devastating spiritual and moral ruin of the human race in Romans 3:10-12, a passage of Scripture taken from Isaiah 52:5 and Ezekiel 36:22: "There is no one righteous, not even one; there is no one who understands, no one who seeks God. All have turned away...there is no one who does good, not even one."

This tragedy of rebellious independence that prompted Adam and Eve to turn away from God is often referred to as "The Fall." The spiritual and moral darkness that ensued because of The Fall pervades all of humanity. It expresses itself in thoughts and actions prompted by a selfish, all-consuming love of self, pride, greed, lust, lying, hatred, fear, insecurity, meanness, cruelty, unforgiveness, bitterness, foolishness, wastefulness, murder, laziness, complacency, the lack of faith (with its eternal perception and pursuit of the eternal things of God, producing a life focused on this fallen, doomed world instead of on God and the lasting things above), and whatever else that is contrary to the holy, loving nature of God and the eternal principles of His kingdom.

One of the most deplorable and saddest consequences of the transfer of allegiance from God to Satan was a severing of family ties to God as His children. Though created by God, people have, by nature, become the children of the devil, subject to the same sentence of damnation—eternal separation from God—as him, their spiritual father.

Intimate friendship and fellowship with God was destroyed because of The Fall—it contaminated what could be called the "spiritual genetic pool" of humanity. Because of Adam and Eve's turning from God, rather than being born with a tendency to serve God, all of their descendants inherited a spiritual nature that is selfish and readily embraces The Lie. Humanity is thus born in sin—spiritually and morally corrupt, polluted, rebellious against God and His authority, and self-centered instead of being holy and God-centered as God had originally intended. Our natural tendency is to either ignore the Lord or give Him only token, religious acknowledgments (that He refuses) while we eagerly run after our own pleasures, plans, purposes, pursuits, and passions.

At its core, Satan's lying offer to Adam and Eve is the same one he has made to all of humanity throughout history and is still being perpetuated by him today. 1 John 2:16 tells us that "...all that is in the world—the lust of the flesh, the lust of the eyes, and the pride of life—come not from the Father but from the world." And who is in charge of the world? According to 1 John 5:19, "...the whole world is under the control and power of the evil one"—Satan. 2 Corinthians 11:14 reveals that he masquerades as an angel of light. From these preceding verses, we realize that Satan—the wicked ruler of this world; the malevolent angel of night—disguises himself as a benevolent angel of light because of his desire to deceive us. He hides himself and his wicked intentions beneath a facade of wisdom and kindness and then appeals to our lusts and pride.

He attempts to persuade us to think that the pathway on which we travel during "the journey" is glorious and leading to self-fulfillment and self-expression, the fullness of happiness, and freedom to follow our desires and do as we please without restraint or consequences. In reality, however, all that he speaks are lies and illusions based on lawlessness. Though often producing momentary earthly pleasures, ultimately, his lying temptations lead those who succumb to him into everlasting destruction. These form a web of deceit that entraps humanity, binding everyone in heavy chains of destructive self-absorption. His evil intentions are to deceptively lead a self-absorbed, clueless, pleasure-and-ego-and-greed-driven humanity down a road of shattered dreams, broken hearts, guilt, seared consciences, wasted lives, gnawing emptiness, futility, maddening frustrations, anger, bitterness, unforgiveness, insatiable, tormenting lusts and habits, and, eventually, to self-destruction and eternal damnation. Self-absorption does surely lead to self-destruction and never-ending torment in Hell.

The Lake Of Fire

Without a miracle of God's mercy and grace, we would all suffer the ultimate penalty of sin, which is the same fate as the one we have so willingly (though sometimes unknowingly) followed—the rebellious Lucifer. That fate is damnation—the curse of eternal separation from God in a place of indescribable, unceasing darkness and torment. According to The Revelation 19:20 and 20:10, this will be "The Lake Of Fire, burning with sulfur and brimstone."

We know that this lake of fire is the final destiny of the damned, for The Revelation 20:14-15 tells us that death and Hell will be thrown into the Lake Of Fire (which is also known as "the second death"). In the Lake Of Fire, all whose names are not found in God's Book of Life when they stand before Him to be judged—those who refused His Son and would not obey Him out of their love for Him—shall fully and forever reap what they have sowed. Having refused the Son of God in life, they will be without Him in death. Rejecting Him in this realm of time will cause them to be rejected by Him in the realm of eternity. Having neglected Him as Lord and Savior now, they shall find Him to be their holy, uncompromising Judge then. Sin, though presently appearing appealing to sinful man, will be stripped of its glamorous masks and be revealed for what it is—a putrefying, unalterable, malignant, spiritual cancer which seeks to infect and consume all that is holy, living, and good. All who embraced sin in this present life shall find it to be a weight that cannot be relinquished in the world to come. It shall pull them down beneath the unrelenting flames of the eternal Lake of Fire. There, the consequence of sin shall be fully realized—unrelenting, unending torment in incomprehensible darkness within a blazing inferno.

Some say that references to a literal, burning place of fire and brimstone filled with the acrid stench of burning sulphur are merely metaphorical. Personally, I don't think so. But, even if they are, believe me, the images conjured at the thoughts of fire, smoke, darkness, stench, undying worms and such (see Mark 9:43-44; The Revelation 14:9-12; 19:20; 20:10-15; and 21:8) probably pale in comparison to the true extent of the horrors and terror that await to fully besiege the damned. After all, remember that in Matthew 25:41, Jesus said that Hell was "prepared for the devil and his angels"—it wasn't even designed for humans(!), but for spiritual creatures filled with all manner of evil and darkness. The residents of the Lake of Fire will probably wish that fire, smoke, and the other images we are given in Scripture were all there was concerning the torments of Hell. Ultimately, the worse part of damnation will be the awareness of having rejected and spurned God's offer of life in his Son, knowing that one is now and forever cut off from God's mercies and concern with no hope of reprieve., O!—such unutterable hopelessness in their unremitting plight will crush down on them forever! We cannot fully imagine just how horrible it is now and will yet be—forever and ever... ... ...

The Deadly, Damning "Disease"

Such a drastic measure is necessary for God to thwart the effects of sin, for, as we've noted, it is like a spiritual, deadly malignancy. This spiritual sickness totally consumes those who refuse to be rid of it. If God did not separate them from the rest of His creation, spiritually "quarantining" them, so to speak, their infectious "disease" would continue to spread, wreaking havoc in all of God's creation, eventually marring everyone and everything in its stark defiance of God and His right to rule.

However, there is an answer for the dilemma of *Our Demise And Deadly Disease*. There is surely a "cure" for this most deadly and devastating of diseases. The "antidote" God provided was the most costly in creation, so costly, in fact, that only God and His Son could pay its price...

3

The Price For The "Cure" From God

*I*n the previous chapter, we considered humanity's spiritual condition that has been brought on by our participation in Lucifer's infectious rebellion. We discussed that this prognosis is terminal and incurable—only a miracle can bring relief and restoration to us.

Thank God, there is a miracle of deliverance and healing available for those willing to admit their condition and who sincerely seek help and a "cure." The only "Specialist" with the "antidote" for sin is God Himself. In His mercy and love, He offers us His precious Son—Jesus Christ—as the one and only, priceless "Cure" for our infection of sin and its ravages. We could never pay for this unfathomable blessing—we must receive Him and His delivering salvation as a gift.

Still, although Christ completed what was needed and necessary to enable us to enjoy fellowship and union with God, this does not mean that there is nothing that He requires of us. God does require something of us if we really desire to be cleansed and set free from this most dreaded of diseases and its ultimate consequence of damnation. [See Ephesians 2:1-4; Romans 8:5-8, 13; The Revelation 20:10-15, etc.]

The Choice We Must Make To Be Chosen

Even though salvation is a gift from God that we cannot possibly earn, we need to remember that many who truly know the Lord (having been chosen by Him to receive salvation) are not further chosen by Him to play important roles in the establishing of His purposes. The reason He does not choose them is because they will not choose Him, keeping Him and His will as the chief focus and joy of their hearts. Since they do not care to make a choice *for* Him and His purposes, the choice is not made *by* Him to bring them into deep fellowship with Himself and to utilize them to further intents that come *from* Him. They have not proven themselves to be faithful and worthy of such a "choosing." Therefore, although we may be His spiritually born again people, what we choose will determine if we are chosen. That is, as His people, we must choose to live in obedience *to* the Lord if we want to be chosen *by* the Lord.

Similarly, in eternity, all of us will stand in The Judgment before God and will receive what we ultimately chose in this present life. Each day, we are pursuing either an ongoing relationship with the Father and Jesus Christ His Son (a relationship that Jesus calls "eternal life" in John 17:3), or our own selfish tendencies and love for this present world (which leads to eternal death).

In Matthew 22:13-14, we read of this reality in an ominous warning from our Lord regarding a coming judgment that will occur during His wedding celebration. At that time, many will be rejected and cast from His presence as He decrees: "Bind him hand and foot, take him away, and cast him into outer darkness; there will be weeping and gnashing of teeth. For many are called, but only a few are chosen."

Again, the reason they will be rejected by the Lord *then* is because they do not choose Him *now*.

If we remain unwilling to love and obey the Lord for the brief breath of a lifetime on the earth, we would not be desirous nor ready to abide in His manifested glory and purity throughout eternity. The standard of measurement for The Judgment is the spiritual and moral perfection of righteousness required by God as set forth in the Law that He gave through Moses. This Law demanded such a complete devotion to God and His ways that all of humanity finds itself unable to live up to it. In fact, just the very first one of "The Ten Commandments" completely does us in. Its high standards stand out in stark contrast to our deplorable and needy state before God. If there was no other law, this commandment alone would justly declare us guilty and worthy of death before God. We find it in Deuteronomy 6:5. There we read, "...you shall love the Lord your God with all your mind and heart, and with your entire being, and with all your might." Who has lived up to such a standard? Who has lived so selflessly and God-focused as to fulfill this command? No one but Jesus Christ. All of us are in total, desperate need of Him. He has stood in our place lest we perish before the holy and just demands of God at The Judgment. Now everyone who will receive His substitutionary sacrifice of Himself for them are freely and fully pardoned. Praise His name!!!

The Requirement, The Message, And The Answer

John 6:28-29 contains a most informative encounter between a group of people and Jesus Christ. They asked Him the ultimate and most important question anyone can ask: "What must we do to carry out what God requires of us?" No other mystery has so captivated the hearts and minds of seekers of truth. All who have ever desired to please God and have longed for relationship with Him have asked in some form or fashion, "What does God require of me? What does He want me to do?"

To many, Jesus' response may come as a shocking surprise. He revealed that anyone who wanted to please God did not have to do anything "religious" in the traditional sense at all:

—He did not challenge them to complete some sort of "holy-grail-type" quest. He sent them on no spiritual trek or down a dark, winding, rabbit trail into their "inner selves."

—He did not tell them to journey to some distant shore, begin some special diet, or flog and afflict themselves with whips, chains, or thorns.

—He pointed them to no so-called "holy place," man-made temple, nor to a religious shrine.

—The Lord did not even prescribe a regimen of religious exercises such as meditating, fasting, praying, reading the Scriptures, or helping others in need. [Not that there is anything wrong with meditating, fasting, praying, reading the Scriptures, or helping others in need. Jesus Himself did these things and instructed His followers to do the same as His Spirit leads them.] However, none of these deeds were given as His answer to this most fundamental and critically important question.

Instead, in John 6:29 we find this simple, bold response from Him, "This is the work (the service) that God asks of you, that you believe in the One Whom He has sent—that you *cleave* to **Me,** trusting, relying on, and having faith in Me, His Messenger."

Notice that believing in Him entails more than merely acknowledging some facts about Him.

The Lord Jesus has made it clear that all of us are to focus on Him—God's Messenger, not simply the words of His message. Actually, that was (and is) *the* message: "Steadfastly cleave to the Lord Jesus alone. Such a relationship and interaction with Him is the only way to have and give true life."

The answer to the mystery we call life is not found in a method or a mantra. It is found in a Man. Not just any man, but the God-Man—Jesus Christ, the Son of the Living God. He proved Himself to be the only perfect substitute to take our place for our rebellion against God for He lived in this physical world without becoming tainted by the rebellion of sin. Rather than yield to its temptations and lies, He steadfastly obeyed His Heavenly Father. Dying on a cross, He took our sin and its resultant death upon Himself. Pouring out His pure and holy soul and blood, He offered Himself as the perfect and final sacrifice as payment for our sin and the sins it produces. Three days later, God raised Him from the dead, giving proof that Jesus had completely satisfied God's standards and demands for perfect holiness and justice. Through His sacrificial death and resurrection, Jesus Christ completely and forever conquered sin, selfishness, Satan, death, Hell, and the grave. Now alive forevermore, He offers us His resurrection life as our only hope and means of victory over all enemies of God and man.

Born Again

Each one of us is desperately in need of God. He is calling to us to open up to Him and be willing to follow His leadings, making the choice to say "Yes!" to Him and allowing Him to place us "in Christ." As John 1:12-13 shows us, "...to all who received and welcomed Jesus Christ—adhering to, trusting in and relying on His name—He gave the right to become the children of God. These are children born not of natural descent, nor of human decision or a husband's will, but born of God." [Also see Romans 8:1; Ephesians 2:6, 10; Colossians 2:10; etc.] And, as we read in 2 Corinthians 5:17, "...if anyone is *in Christ*, he is a new creation; old things have passed away; behold, all things have become new." This is what it means to be "born again." It is not a physical rebirth, and neither is it just a mental or emotional change of perspective.

It is literally a transforming rebirth and re-creation of one's heart or spirit (also known as our "inner man" or "the hidden man of the heart"). This is that part of us designed to be the place of God's abode within us and from where He intended to lead and direct us. However, because of sin, it became "dead" (insensitive and unresponsive) to God. Through the working of the Holy Spirit in us and our yielded responsiveness to Him in repentance and in turning to God, it becomes reborn, alive, and responsive to Him. Thus, in the depths of our being we are truly "born again." These wonderful realties of the New Covenant were prophesied in the Old in Ezekiel 36:26 and Jeremiah 17:9.

God desires that we believe Him and love Him. True love *for* Him and trust *in* Him will be demonstrated through our dependency *on* Him so that by the power of the Spirit sent *from* Him we can faithfully live in obedience *to* Him.

The Choice To Pay The Cost

Until and unless we repent (meaning "to change our mind and thus, our life's direction; turning from sin to do God's will") His perfect, holy justice finds us all guilty and condemned as willing participants in the world system and its rebellion against Him. If we really desire to walk with Him in His fullness of life, free from the torments of a guilty conscience and the fear of a justly painful "payback," we must make the choice to follow Him wholeheartedly. This means we will have to renounce the rebellious nature and trust God's Spirit to replace it with Christ's own perfect, God-pleasing nature. All demand and pursuit of self-rule must be forsaken if we desire to know God's rule in our lives.

Jesus Christ—our only hope of salvation—gave His all and He requires our all. To truly experience salvation, we must believe in—that is: receive, trust in, and cling to—the substitutionary sacrifice that He willingly made on our behalf when He poured out His life and blood for us on the cross. In John 14:6, He said, "I am the way, the truth, and the life. No one comes to the Father except through Me." In John 3:16, He reveals that God loves us so much that He sent Him to earth so that whoever will cling to Him as their hope and very life will not perish. Instead, they will enjoy relationship and fellowship with God forever. They will be reborn spiritually, becoming one of God's children. Yes, it is a "free" gift, but one that we cannot receive while grasping anything else. Although "free" in the sense that we cannot earn it and God gives it to us without our having to merit it, it will "cost" us *everything.* That is, to be able to cling to Jesus, we must stop clinging to all else. All of our trust is to be put in Him, His faithfulness, His Word, and His nature, and all of our love is to be set on Him and God the Father. Only then can we enjoy relationship with the Lord, cleansed and safe from the power and penalty of the sinful Rebellion. And only then can we walk in the reality of His delivering, enabling, saving power moment to moment.

God has no grandkids. Salvation cannot be "passed down" genetically or bequeathed to others. We must experience God for ourselves, becoming born again spiritually by His Spirit. We will not get in to the marriage supper of the Lamb on someone else's coattails. Each one of us must personally have our own encounter and ongoing relationship with God.

Sceva's Sons' Run

We must have our *own* testimony, as The Revelation 12:11 tells us. There we read that all who overcome the devil will do so by the blood of the lamb, the word or utterance of their testimony, and they will not love and cling to life even when faced with death. Notice that it says "the word of *their* testimony," not the word of someone else's testimony. Our testimony is born out of our own personal, genuine experience and moment by moment walk with God. Others' testimonies may stir us and encourage us, but the knowledge of someone else's experience does not give us our own.

This reminds me of the account of the sons of a man named "Sceva," recorded in Acts 19:13-16. They were not disciples of Jesus Christ because they had never confessed Him as their Lord. They had not accepted the saving, substitutionary work of His death and resurrection. Nevertheless, these exorcists tried to use His name and authority to cast demons out of people afflicted with them. According to the Scriptures, "...some of the itinerant Jewish exorcists took it upon themselves to call the name of the Lord Jesus over those who had evil spirits, saying, 'In the name of Jesus, Whom Paul preaches, I command you to come out.' Seven sons of Sceva, a

Jewish chief priest, were doing this. But one day, an evil spirit answered them, 'Jesus I know, and Paul I know about, but who are you?' Then the man who had the evil spirit jumped on them and overpowered them all. He gave them such a beating that they ran out of the house naked and bleeding."

They had tried to spiritually "trade" on the name of Jesus as though it was some form of spiritual exchange or had some kind of spiritually marketable value, much like gold coins are used in the financial world of man. But, although they used the name of Jesus when dealing with some demoniacs, they had not first "come to Him" in submission to Him as their Lord and Savior. We know this to be true because John 6:45 records Jesus Himself having said, "Everyone who listens to the Father and learns from Him comes to Me." Rather than speaking as those who had "come to" the Lord and developed a genuine relationship with Him, the way they referenced the Lord revealed that they were at best only aware of Jesus in some kind of distant, detached way—"the Jesus Whom *Paul* preaches," not as the Jesus *they* preached from experiential knowledge.

Sceva's sons spoke of and knew *about* the Jesus Whom Paul preached, but they did not *know Him*, at least not in the way each of us must know Him in order to be considered one of His people. Perhaps they had personally met the Lord during His life on earth, perhaps not. But, regardless, they had never really come to know Him in the way He intended by submitting their all to Him and acknowledging Him as their Lord and Savior. The authority and power of Jesus was not theirs to use because they had no spiritual relationship with Him. They had not yet been willing to receive the revelation from the Holy Spirit of Who Jesus Christ really is— the Messiah, the Son of the Living God. Because of this, they had no spiritual authority over the devil, no matter how much they attempted to use the name of Jesus like some kind of magical mantra or piece of merchandise.

They did not have their own testimony which develops only as someone accepts the sacrifice of the blood of Jesus the Lamb of God and then lives daily in submission to Him by relying on the power of His Holy Spirit.

This cost them dearly. Defeat was certain because, although they spoke right words, they had wrong hearts—their so-called "testimony" was "phoney baloney."

Had they really belonged to God, *they* would have opened their hearts and welcomed the One Whom He sent, thereby experiencing spiritual transformation and impartation of authority from Christ. They would have not merely tried to use His name as though it was merely part of an incantation. In John 8:43 and 47, Jesus said to a group of people, "Why do you not understand what I am saying? Because you are unable to hear what I say...Whoever belongs to God listens to God.—Those who belong to God hear the words of God. This is the reason that you do not listen, because you do not belong to God."

[Understand that when our Lord speaks of hearing His words, He not only means that we perceive what He is communicating to us, but that we obey what He says. After all, the people He was so pointedly rebuking in this passage were hearing Him in a physical sense, but they were not willing to obey Him. Therefore, we see that disobeying Him and not hearing Him are synonymous.]

Our Lord said in John 5:23, "Whoever does not honor the Son does not honor the Father Who sent Him." And 1 John 2:22-23 contains the following blunt, scathing words: "Who is the liar? It is the one who denies that Jesus is the Christ—the Messiah. Such a person is antiChrist, denying the Father and the Son. No one who denies the Son has the Father; whoever acknowledges the Son has the Father also."

The Walk—Just Talk?

We're either genuinely God's children who are miraculously born again and have it settled in our hearts to live in obedience to Him through the power of His Holy Spirit, or we are fakes and children of the devil. Living right—not merely talking right—will reveal to whom we belong. As our Lord said in John 8:44 to certain people who, according to verse thirty-one, *"had believed on Him,"* "Your father is the devil, and you do exactly what he wants." They had some correct information in their heads, but they had not experienced the transformation of their hearts that comes only through submission and devotion to Jesus Christ.

Each one of us needs to ask ourself:

- Is my so-called *"walk with* God merely *talk about* God?
- Am I merely being *in*formed *about* God,
  or am I really being *trans*formed *by* God?
- Have I *genuinely* met the Lord?
- Am I growing in my love for Him?
- Is my claim of love for Him and relationship with Him evident to me *and* others by the choices I make? That is, do I live in obedience to His Word, or am I someone who merely *professes* to be a disciple of Christ, but not one who truly *possesses* the life of God?
- Do I have an ongoing, real, personal knowledge and awareness of Him, or is my faith merely a sham, a fake, a put-on based only on the testimonies and experiences of others? In other words, do I have a genuine, personal faith of my own, or a superficial, fake, so called "hand-me-down-faith?"
- Do I have a genuine relationship *with* God,
  or merely religion *about* Him?
- Do I claim loyalty to God simply because I was taught that I should, yet my mind and heart remain uncertain, neither committed?
- Is my profession of being a follower of Jesus Christ only a front for gaining or maintaining the approval and praise of certain people?
- Is my claim to belong to Jesus Christ perhaps only an attempt to quiet a guilty and condemning conscience while I choose to live independently of God in disobedience to Him?
- Do I persistently pursue sin?
- When I sin, am I quick to repent *and* forsake it?
- Do I genuinely struggle against sin, or do I merely "huff 'n' puff" in an effort to convince myself and others that I struggle against sin (when, in actuality, i don't)?
- In an effort to please God, walk in holiness, and hate evil, is any apparent struggle on my part against sin genuine, or am I just putting on a showy front in an effort to cover a deceitful, unrepentant, sin-loving heart?

• Am I merely a student who is only learning about Jesus Christ, or am I truly a disciple of Jesus Christ who does what He desires?

In 1 John 2:29 we read that everyone "...who practices righteousness is born of Him." 1 John 3:4-10 tells us that "...sin is lawlessness. But you know that Jesus Christ, in Whom is no sin, appeared so that He might take away our sins. No one who lives in Him deliberately and knowingly habitually commits or practices sin. No one who habitually sins has either seen or known Him. Dear children, do not let anyone lead you astray. Whoever lives a consistently conscientious life, practicing righteousness, is righteous, just as He is righteous. He who practices evil doing is of the devil, because the devil has been sinning from the beginning. The reason the Son of God appeared was to destroy the devil's work [of sinning against God—LT]. No one who is born of God habitually practices sin, because God's seed remains in him; he cannot go on sinning, because he has been born of God. This is how we know who the children of God are and who the children of the devil are: Anyone who does not do what is right is not a child of God; nor is anyone who does not love his brother."

In Matthew 7:26 and 27, our Lord made it clear that those who are pleasing to Him are those who *do* His will, not those who merely *know* His will. Becoming disciples of Jesus requires that we turn *from sin* so that we can turn *to Him* and actively pursue Him and the doing of His will. This is why in The Revelation 2:5 He exhorted the Ephesian believers to repent and *do* those things which they had done when they first believed on Him. He didn't merely want them to confess their sins to Him. He also wanted them to forsake their sins and follow through with righteous living— *doing* His will, not merely *talking* about it.

Many of us may find these things disturbing, but the Spirit of God can use them to expose the true condition of our hearts. As He does, He gives us the opportunity to strengthen within us all we have received from Him and to repent of those things that are not of Him. When the Lord draws near to us, the brilliance of His holy light reveals sinful darkness within us—a revelation of self accompanies a revelation of God.

Spiritual Poverty "Exchanged" For God's Rich Mercy & Grace!

We see this in Isaiah 6:1-8. There we read that Isaiah cried out in self-loathing and shame as a specific wickedness in his heart was exposed in the overwhelmingly holy Presence of God. Times like these that are so very revealing are extremely difficult, even painful at times. Nevertheless, the revealing of Himself to us with its accompanying trauma is an act of His love to enable an ongoing revelation of Himself within our hearts.

If these words have caused you to recognize a deplorable condition of heart within you, know that you are not alone. We are all a mess apart from Jesus. Left on our own, by our strength, none of us could begin to live up to the standard of holiness that is revealed by John to be the requirement of discipleship. All of us desperately need the holy Presence and power of God to be at work in us giving us both the desire and ability to do God's will. It is only through the working of the Holy Spirit in our lives (with our willing cooperation) that we are enabled to walk in holiness as God desires.

So do not allow the enemy to use even a God-given insight to your neediness as a means of pulling you into a downward spiral of permanent despair. Though it is true that, in the presence of God, we, like Isaiah, will be exposed for the rogues that we all are apart form His intervening mercy and grace, be comforted in the knowledge that, also like Isaiah, we can find cleansing, mercy, and help from the holy God of redemption and burning love.

Thank God for His unfathomable and committed love for us!

Be assured that He delights in helping weak ones who know they need His strength, sinners who long to be transformed by His mercy and grace into saints, yes, He delights in all who depend exclusively upon Him to overcome the trials, tests, and temptations of life. Just be certain that you keep before you the fact that, if we truly desire to walk in *God's* ways, we must lay aside *our* ways. Our plans, purposes, passions, preconceptions, and pursuits must be forsaken if we are to deeply know and experience Him and His will. All religion *about* the Lord must be forsaken if we are to experience relationship *with* the Lord. Through dependency on the Lord Jesus and obedience to His Word and His Holy Spirit, we are able to fulfill the ultimate purpose for living—to bring joy to God's heart by loving, knowing, and obeying Him.

Let's open our hearts to Him as we turn from sin to pursue Him and His ways diligently. Forgiven, we can praise and worship Him in sincerity and truth. As we get a glimpse of what we deserve and what He did to set us free, we are filled with delight and wonder: Delight with Him for being so kind and generous, and wonder that He would be this way with us.

Apart from His wonderful, transforming love, mercy, and powerful grace, all of us would remain God-defying anarchists, hopelessly and helplessly lost, destined for Hell and the Lake of Fire. But now, because of His kindness, we can forever share with Him His victory. Jesus Christ has paid the price to set us all free from our demise and the deadly "disease" of sin. We simply must accept and receive *The Price For the "Cure" From God.*

Know that Jesus has already died for all of your sins. He knows you, loves you, and accepts you. Don't prolong your agony and His as well by hanging on to "bummed out" feelings of worthlessness and uselessness. These are tools of Satan to beat you up and drag you down. Remind yourself and the devil that God loved you so much that, even before you knew Him, He loved you and gave His son to die in your place. Instead of staying in a an emotional and spiritual state of feeling bad about yourself for your failures and defeats, be joyful and full of grateful praise to Jesus for His triumphant, sin-and-self-and-devil-conquering love and grace. Instead of putting yourself down, lift Jesus up!

[The following contains graphic descriptions of the torture and death suffered by Jesus Christ. Reader discretion is advised, particularly if reading to younger children.]

Come, let me show you how to be forever remembered by the Lord…

—4—

Lord, Remember Me

*I*t had all happened so fast…

There had been a trial, if you could call it a trial. In actuality, the bitter, biased, kangaroo court had trodden truth and jurisprudence underfoot. Like a ravenous beast stealthily stalking its prey, the self-righteous judge and jury had eagerly awaited this moment, and now they would settle for nothing less than this man's blood. Through the breach of numerous standards of righteousness and of lawful trial procedures, a wrongly contrived verdict based on false accusations, lies, and deceit had been reached—"guilty for treason against the government and blasphemy against God."

The sentence—*death!*

The method of execution—crucifixion.

The sooner, the better.

Then, before the penalty was carried out, the man's accusers and judges actually spit in his face and struck him with their fists. During this humiliating travesty, they never stopped sarcastically mocking and taunting him.

A short time later, the condemned man was flogged mercilessly with a whip called "a cat-of-nine-tails." It consisted of multiple leather straps that had bits of bone, glass, and lead attached to their ends. The straps dug deeply as they chewed up a body—tearing and shredding flesh, muscle, blood vessels, and even ripping out pieces of bone. The wounds inflicted were horrible, reducing those beaten this way to a bleeding, shredded, nearly unrecognizable pulp. So traumatizing and damaging was such torture that many a person died under these lashes of death.

Then a whole army battalion was gathered together to make sadistic sport of the condemned man, compounding his humiliation and pain. Three hundred tough, war-hardened Roman soldiers—seasoned in tactics of cruelty—threw a robe around his bloody shoulders and made a cap or "crown" of thorns—sharp and several inches long—that they put on his head, causing great pain and profuse bleeding. Bowing down in a mockery of his claim to be a king, they beat him, struck him in the face, spit on him, plucked out his beard, and bashed the "crown" deeply into his skull by hitting him on his head again and again with a heavy stick. After tiring of their degrading games, they stripped him, reopening the wounds inflicted by the flogging, put his own clothes back on him, and led him away to be crucified.

At the summit of a macabre, menacing-looking hill, the sentence was carried out with ruthless and deadly precision. The condemned man was thrown upon the roughly hewn timbers of a wooden cross. His arms were then extended outward from his body and one foot was placed on top of the other...

Wham!

The man's eyes opened wide as he cried out in indescribable, convulsing pain.

Wham! Wham!! Wham!!!

With brutal force, large, long, and crude nails were pounded through the man's wrists and feet into the cross, fastening him to it. With each blow, gut-wrenching pain was sent through his body. Nerve endings screamed in protest, and fiery shock waves of torment exploded in his brain.

Soon, this part of the soldiers' grim and grisly job was completed. They then lifted the cross and, with a heavy *thud,* secured it in an upright position. The condemned man hung there, a bruised, bleeding, dying silhouette suspended between earth and a rumbling, rapidly darkening sky—as this tragic scene unfolded, all of nature seemed to convulse, painfully retching in protest.

On either side of this man, two other condemned men were also crucified. All three painfully struggled to breathe as they bled and suffocated in the clutches of one of the most painful and inhumane means of death ever devised.

In fact, our most descriptive word for intense pain—"excruciating"—is a derivative of "out of the cross" or "crucified." Joints were pulled out of place. Feelings of insatiable thirst became overwhelming. Labored, gasping breaths could be taken only by pushing up on the nails in the feet because this was the only way to enable the diaphragm to work, allowing the lungs to expand. This tormented nerves and bones in the feet, sending screaming shock waves of excruciating pain throughout the body.

Due to the severe beatings and flogging he had received, this was especially distressing for this particular man. For every time he wanted to breathe, he had to rub his mangled back up and down over the rough-hewn timbers.

Gradually, the lungs and heart would become filled with blood and other body fluids. Eventually, death would claim another victim as those who were crucified either drowned in their own juices or their hearts would burst.

Those in the crowd who had cried out for the death of the man in the middle had felt swept up in a swelling tide of mob-like frenzy. Some of them calmed a bit as their eyes beheld the result of their unrelenting, bloodthirsty cries for his death. There were many, however, who remained in a furious, irrational uproar. Even as they gazed at this pitiful, sickening spectacle of humiliation and torture, their crazed and raging hatred for this man was not appeased. Instead, it was incensed...

"Hey, you fool! Where are your followers now?" they bitterly shouted. "You saved others, but you can't save yourself! Come down off your cross and we'll believe in you. You *claimed* to be Messiah and the Son of God, so let's see if God will save you now. If He does, we'll fall down and worship you. But you know as well as we do, you fake, that He ain't gonna help you one bit. The show's over—it's curtain time, loser! Ha-ha-ha!!!" On and on they went...cursing and mocking this man...spitting on him...taunting him...hurting him...

Nearly everyone present seemed to be caught-up in the insanity and unfairness of that moment. From paupers to priests and children to the aged, it seemed as though the whole world was against this one man. Even those crucified with him hurled bitter insults through their clenched teeth and searing pain.

For a while, that is...

From Reviling To Reveling; Revulsion To Revelation; Rejection To Redemption

For soon, one of the criminals began to take notice of the demeanor of the one immediately beside him. He watched as this pitiable, pitiful creature responded to the crowd's venomous hate and disdain with unfeigned kindness, even love. No matter how cruel the taunts, no matter how loud the blasphemous cries were against the man in the middle, he never retaliated. The criminal marveled as he even heard this man lift a prayer to God on behalf of his murderers: "Father, forgive them, for they don't know what they're doing."

What??? the criminal thought to himself, not understanding why nor how such gracious words could come from the figure beside him. He torturously turned his head to look with curiosity and amazement at the Man—Yeshua Ben Joseph of Nazareth—Who suffered next to him.

Look at what they've done to him—what a bloody mess— he doesn't even look human, the criminal thought to himself. As the crowd continued hurling their blasphemous insults at Yeshua, the convict began to ponder the tragic irony of the situation.

*"If this doesn't beat all. What injustice! Just look at 'em—a bunch of low-down, lyin' hypocrites; a dirty, filthy pack of hungry wolves. What has this man ever done to deserve anything like this? Nothing! Everything I ever heard about him was good. It's this murdering crowd of hypocrites and sinners that oughta be up here. They should be on a cross, not him. **They're** the ones that deserve to die. **I** deserve to die. But not **him.***

As time passed, he felt what seemed like waves of shame engulf him, not so much for the shame of crucifixion or for even the crime that put him there. Instead, he was feeling a growing sense of utter unworthiness to be even in the presence of the man beside him. For, although he was in such vile circumstances, he nonetheless seemed to radiate a sort of regal majesty.

The criminal slowly turned his head, again scanning the throbbing scene of insanity before him. He watched in horror as the crowd drew closer to Yeshua, jeering and laughing at him with such scorn and evil intent that the criminal was amazed. At times, there were unearthly shrieks and even what sounded like ferocious howls coming from the crowd. The very atmosphere was eerie, evil, and deeply disturbing. *What's goin' on? I've seen lots of crucifixions, but this one is different—totally different. There's only one way to describe it,* he thought. *More than anything I've ever known, this looks and feels like a scene from the depths of Hell.* He hung his head and tightly shut his eyes, hoping somehow to block out the overwhelming sense of injustice and evil he was sensing in the air and feeling in the pit of his stomach.

For some reason that he couldn't completely understand, he was growing more and more uneasy. He felt as if he was witnessing something of mammoth proportions; something of great, unfathomable destiny and historical significance. It was as if he had been unknowingly and unwillingly cast to play an insignificant role in a great epic that was unfolding around him. He was beginning to feel as though he had gone out on stage before his cue, unprepared and even unworthy to be a part of the drama. Simultaneously, the one next to him was on center stage before an audience of heaven and earth, gloriously fulfilling the star role for which he was born. A role he alone could do.

The sky grew darker and darker, evermore ominous and threatening, finally becoming pitch black. *Can you believe it?* the criminal thought to himself. *Even the sun is refusing to shine. What in the world is happening?* Suddenly, there was a bright flash of lightning, followed by a deafening thunderclap— *crrraaaaaaaaack...boooOOOooom!!!* A deep rumble from the heavens shook the earth, making it feel as though the foundations of creation itself were being removed. The wind increased, sounding like it was crying and wailing a mournful funeral dirge. The crowd was noticeably frightened and became more subdued. Many even began to comment that God was not pleased at what was taking place there. Quickly, they began to leave the hellish scene to return to their homes, nervously desiring yet not finding a sense of security, solace, and comfort after witnessing the ghastly and horrid events of the last several hours.

But in the midst of this nightmarish setting, when it seemed as though the world was coming to a frightening end, something was being birthed in the heart and mind of the contemplative criminal condemned to die with Yeshua...

He began to sense light instead of darkness.

Life in place of death.

Hope in the chasm of despair.

And he suddenly became aware of a gnawing hunger and thirst in the center of his being that was much deeper than the physical pangs of hunger and thirst that he was feeling.

From within this criminal there arose deep, heartfelt questions and conclusions...

The crowd was screaming that Yeshua claimed to be Messiah. *What if it's true?* His mind was racing. *Could He possibly be the One Israel has been waiting for? The prophet Daniel prophesied that Messiah would come in these very days. The rabbis tell us that Messiah would come during the existence of the second temple, the one that's standing now. And no one has ever done the miracles this man has done. No one has ever helped or cared for others the way He has in these past few years. Who but Messiah could do these things?*

Yet now he's dying...

But...didn't the Torah reveal that the Prince—the Messiah—would be cutoff—killed? Didn't the 53rd chapter of Isaiah describe the death of Messiah, revealing that He would bear our guilt and punishment for our sins against the Holy God?

In his heart, a spark of truth had begun to ignite a flame of revelation and conviction that was growing brighter and stronger. He looked at the sign above the head of the Man beside him. It read, "YESHUA OF NAZARETH—THE KING OF THE JEWS."

I think they got that right. Who else but this Man has even come close to fulfilling the many prophecies concerning Messiah? I remember John—the man they called "the Baptizer"— spoke of this man Yeshua, pointing Him out and calling Him the Lamb sent from God Who takes away the sin of the world. I know that the name "Yeshua" means "God saves," or "Salvation is of the Lord." Perhaps this One beside me has been sent by Yahweh to save His people. Could I actually be witnessing the final sacrifice, the death of The Last Lamb? Could I actually be hanging right next to the Holy One, the Son of the Living God?

Yes!!! This Man, Yeshua of Nazareth, is Yeshua—the Messiah of Israel! He is truly our King!!!

And just as Isaiah prophesied that Messiah would die, he also prophesied that somehow, Messiah would live again...

His thoughts were abruptly interrupted by another spiteful tirade of words directed at Yeshua from the other man condemned to die with them:

"Yeshua! If you are Messiah, then do something!!! Prove to everyone who you are by saving yourself. And save us, too, while you're at it!"

The other criminal, now repentant, could no longer tolerate the injustice and defamation being heaped on the Man next to him. Someone had to speak out for this innocent One:

"Hey!!! Don't you even fear God when you are dying? We deserve to die for the wicked things that we've done. We had it comin' to us. But this Man has done *nothing wrong!!!*"

The other criminal turned away, angry and humiliated, but silenced for the moment.

Yet, now that he had begun to speak, the criminal with the change of heart and mind felt compelled to continue. His newly discovered insight and the conviction in his heart had to be expressed. So much of his life had been wasted. So many wrongs and been committed and so many opportunities for good had been squandered. He would not make that mistake now. Even though each word required all of his concentration and extreme effort, and though he was on the verge of physical death, he lifted his weary head once again to speak to the One he now knew could somehow give to him forgiveness for his God-defying selfishness. He was convinced that Yeshua could grant him eternal life—the grave would not be the end of existence. So, through parched, dying lips, he spoke words of longing, of faith, and of hope. Words of commitment and trust. In so doing, he placed his entire, eternal destiny on the mercies and the power of Yeshua.

"Lord..."

*Yes—**LORD**. This Man called Yeshua of Nazareth is Lord. The Messiah of God. The Savior of the world. The Promised One for Whom the Jewish nation for centuries had prayed to God to send to deliver them from their enemies. And what greater enemy was there than the taskmaster known as "sin"?*

The repentant criminal beside Him was one of those precious souls of the harvest who are willing to receive the revelation from God concerning Who Jesus is—the King of God's heavenly kingdom. He was one of the relatively few who listen to God and feel that He is even worth the knowing. Most choose instead to listen to others or to follow the faulty reasonings of their own minds, never seeing beyond this present, temporal realm, and living unaware of the eternal realm of God's kingdom. But this man was enabled to look beyond the physical appearance of Jesus. He saw Jesus as more than merely someone beaten mercilessly, bloody, pitiful, weak, dying, and rejected by his peers. By the mercy and the grace of God, the condemned man saw and recognized that Jesus Christ was more than a mere man. He realized that Jesus was God's Man, sent from Heaven to bring back to God all who would depend upon Him for salvation. With practically his dying breath, the convict declared with his mouth and chose to believe in his heart the revelation from God that Jesus is the Messiah—the Christ—the King of God's invisible, heavenly kingdom. He began to realize that Yeshua haMashiach—Jesus the Messiah— was his only hope, source of forgiveness, help, and comfort.

"...remember me when You come into Your kingdom."

There.

It was said.

All of his eternal hopes and dreams had been cast upon the One next to him. The man had found, in this place of death, the Source of life. Now he waited for His response.

Time seemed to stand still as Yeshua turned his head to return the gaze of the repentant man. The man momentarily forgot his pain and the looming specter of death as he gazed into the gentle eyes of the Savior—the Lamb of God sent from God to take away the sin of the world.

His eyes were piercing yet accepting.

Knowing but forgiving.

Fiery and holy, yet comforting and enabling.

Pools of searching, holy love.

Father's Gift—Christ's Crisis

What a thrill and a comfort this man's insightful and humble request must have been for the Lord "Jesus" (a gentile derivation of "Yeshua," His Hebrew name). At this time of such unimaginable agony and despair, what an encouraging gift from His Father it must have been to have beside Him one who was being transformed through faith. Yeshua had come to establish on the earth a people who lived in perception and pursuit of things other than the physical realm. And now, in the most unlikely of places, hanging on a cross beside him, was a reminder from His Father that His mission was not in vain. He would look on the travail of His soul and be satisfied, knowing that His Father would be pleased and a people would be brought back into relationship with God through the shedding of His sinless blood on their behalf.

Perhaps, after the man spoke, the Son of God closed His eyes for a few moments and turned His face upward...

He sees, Father. He sees! He has heard You speak deep within him concerning Me and My eternal, invisible Kingdom, and He's beginning to realize Who I am and why You sent Me to earth. Here is one who has realized His need of coming home to the ways of truth, My Father, and is willing to acknowledge Me as King and serve Me with love. Oh, thank You, Abba. Praise Your mighty, holy, eternal Name!

Then, with a penetrating, accepting gaze that went deep into the man's very soul, the Lord spoke. With sincerity and conviction, Jesus responded to the man's repentant, heartfelt cry, bringing peace and comfort to the dying man's soul. For, as the condemned man saw and acknowledged Who Jesus Christ really is, he partook of Christ's mercies and was given the ultimate pardon, "I tell you the truth, today you will be with Me in Paradise." [See Matthew 26-28; Mark 14-16; Luke 22-24; John 18-21.] Soon afterwards, both of them died.

Imagine what may have transpired after death:

There they are in Paradise. Free from pain. Free from rejection. Free from the taunting crowd. Free from damnation. I can picture the man enjoying the reality of his being cleansed from sin by the very blood he had watched run down Jesus' cross only moments before. Recognizing the Savior and turning to Him, the man asks somewhat tentatively, "Lord, remember me?"

I can see the Lord turn to look at him. Recognizing the man, He breaks forth in a huge smile as tears of joy begin running down His cheeks. Stretching out His arms, He enthusiastically embraces and tightly hugs His forgiven follower and brother. Then, with great joy and without hesitation, the Lord Jesus replies, "Oh, yes, My friend, My little brother. I remember you!"

Where Do You Stand?

Each one of us can find ourselves represented in this saga that occurred some two thousand years ago. Do you see yourself easily fitting among the judge and jury that condemned Jesus Christ to die? Like them, have you become smug in your interpretations of Scripture, therefore hardening your heart to the Holy Spirit's revelation of God's word?

Be honest with yourself and with God.

Have you shut out the dealings of His Holy Spirit because of spiritual pride, refusing to acknowledge the Truth He is desirous to reveal to you? Are you like the religious leaders who condemned Jesus in that you are most focused on your own desires than on

God and His desires? You may have tender, appreciative emotions arise within you as you think of what Christ accomplished on the cross, but have you ever willingly embraced the Christ of the cross, acknowledging Him as your Lord and Savior? Are you desirous of relationship *with* God, or merely religion *about* God? Are you destitute in spirit because you have substituted other things, maybe even religious things, for an ongoing relationship and fellowship with God Himself? Do you think of relationship with God primarily as a means to get things *from* Him, or are you genuinely interested in a relationship *with* Him? Are you, like the religious court that condemned Jesus, concerned about how He will affect your heritage, religious traditions, and social standing rather than willingly submitting to Him as Lord and Messiah? You may claim to know the truth, but remember, truth without love becomes letter without life—merely dead, religious dogma—and love without truth is quickly perverted into carnal sensuality.

Then again, perhaps you see yourself in the crowd, convinced that those in authority are right, regardless of whether they walk in truth and in love. Are you swayed by the multitudes, "following the crowd," living your life according to what others may think, do, or say? Do you live for the approval and praise of people, or of God?

Or, do you listen to what others say, yet still think for yourself, knowing that God holds each of us individually responsible for the decisions that we make, regardless of what others may say or what they think of us? We must carefully weigh the things that we are told, whether from those in authority or not. Examination of what they say in light of Scripture should and can be done without resisting the authority that God has given them.

Have you, like many prejudiced ones in the crowd, found solace and an ease of conscience in the thought that you have a "good, respectable" heritage? Is cockiness because of your "roots" blinding you to the barrenness of your own soul? Regardless of our backgrounds, if we do not invite the Risen, Living Christ to dwell within our hearts, we are in unfathomable danger and need. Although we may have much worldly wealth and prestige among our peers, the divine decree is: Without Jesus Christ, we are lost and without hope.

Maybe you are among those who have heard of Him, but are just too busy or indifferent to care about Him or that which He came to proclaim. You sacrifice the eternal for the sake of the temporal—forsaking that which is lasting for that which is fleeting. Like folks that are spiritually hard of hearing and blind, do you drown God's voice and eradicate His reality from your perception in a constant bombardment of distractions? Is your time consumed with meaningless chatter, radio, TV, magazines, novels, or a thousand other things and passing fads that clamor for your attention and dull your sense of perceiving and pursuing what is lasting and really important? Is God crowded out of your life with the busyness and business of everyday existence? Are you even caught-up in things (such as family, career, good works, etc.) that perhaps are not wicked in and of themselves, yet have become idols because they occupy a place in your heart that was created for God alone, things that seem to be "good" but have taken the place of "God" in your heart?

Then again, maybe you are like the rough and tough soldiers, carrying out with perfunctory duty the tasks that others tell you to do, regardless of whether those tasks are honorable or not. Have you, like many of these soldiers, seen and inflicted so much pain that your heart has grown callous? Have you had a difficult time appreciating what is directly in front of you, just as these soldiers did not recognize Who they were abusing and killing? Do you, like them, even tend to despise and attempt to destroy the very thing that can give you life?

Or, are you like the other criminal who was crucified with Jesus? He cursed the Lord and apparently never repented of this or any of his other sins. His heart was completely self-centered. He didn't care a thing about Jesus Christ or the interests of Christ's eternal kingdom. He did not desire to recognize Jesus Christ as Lord. Instead, he only wanted Jesus to help him out of his predicament.

Sadly, multitudes today are in the same condition of heart. They are missing the eternal focus of Christ's coming and kingdom because they are so caught-up in their own selfish pursuits that they are not willing to deny themselves so that they can lay hold of God and His purposes.

Most of us try to use Jesus for our own plans, purposes, schemes, and scams. Unfortunately, however, whenever we set our hearts on things that are temporary and of this earth, we sacrifice that which is eternal and belonging to the kingdom of God. Whoever would please God must have faith—the God-given ability to perceive and the willingness to pursue the unseen things of His eternal kingdom, hidden from our natural eyes and senses. We must live for the realities of the eternal, invisible world to come, not for this world or for the things that are on the earth. Then and only then can we live with a proper focus and purpose in this present life.

Whenever we lose our perception and pursuit of the eternal, unseen things of God's kingdom, the Lord Jesus is greatly saddened, for, as Hebrews 11:6 reveals, without faith it is impossible to please God. If we really desire to please the Lord and lay hold of the unseen things of His kingdom, we need to stop setting our hearts on things that we can see and will soon perish forever.

Profession Without Possession

There are many who consider themselves Christians—reading their Bibles, praying, and ministering to others—who are not really "born again." They may have good morals, but they have never been convicted of their sin of living independently of God. They profess much, but possess little. They say good things, but live the wrong way because of a wrong center and focus.

Remember, Jesus told us in John 3:3 that unless someone is born again, that person can never see the kingdom of God, which is the will of the Father fully and perfectly expressed. And many who claim to know the Lord don't see the kingdom of God. His will is not their chief concern and delight. Instead, their own agenda is. They are not willing to turn from a selfish life of temporal pursuits and interests to give themselves completely to the Lord for the fulfillment of His eternal purposes, pursuits, and plans. Rather, they have merely tried to add God to their self-centered life.

They have never been smitten in their hearts by the conviction that everyone is born in sin—born as rebellious sinners who love selfishness and their own ways rather than God and His ways, thus deserving to be cutoff from Him forever. Mankind was created to know God, love God, and obey God, but we all have turned from Him and gone our own way, choosing to do our own thing rather than obeying God.

Though many may very well be outwardly moral and even well-respected by "the moral majority" does not mean that they have become part of "the repentant minority" who have turned from their own ways to the Lord Jesus, giving Him absolute rulership over their lives. They may even be very involved in *Church*ianity— all that is popularly thought of as Christian or "church"-related activities—but that does not mean that they have experienced *Christ*ianity—a genuine relationship and ongoing fellowship with Jesus Christ Himself.

Our Lord tells us in John 14:21 that He will reveal Himself intimately to those who obey Him. In John 17:3, He says that eternal life is to know the only true God and Jesus Christ Whom He has sent. And in 1 John 2:4, we read, "He who says, 'I know Him,' and does not do what He commands, is a liar, and the truth is not in him." By putting the messages of these three Scripture verses together, we can conclude that whoever refuses to obey God rejects God; all who refuse to follow Him in this life will not partake of eternal life—they will not intimately know God and Jesus Christ His Son. Having refused to love and follow Christ in this life, they will face an eternity without Him—whoever refuses and rejects Him in this present life will be refused entrance into His eternal kingdom and will be rejected by Him in the life to come. This will occur on The Day Of Judgment when each person will give an account of his or her life to God.

THE Marriage—NOW!

So we see that we do not belong to Christ unless we truly encounter Him by the revelation of His Spirit, submit fully to His lordship, give ourselves to Him, and choose to purse knowing Him intimately. It has been said that our relationship with Jesus NOW is one of marriage—that the marriage supper of the Lamb in the life to come follows the wedding that takes place between us and our Divine Husband *now. Now*—in this life and at this moment— we are to come into full union with Him—*now* are we to forsake all other spiritual "dates" and "lovers" and be a chaste, dedicated bride for Jesus Christ—*now* are we considered to be adulterous if we "flirt" and cajole sin, just as James 4:4 sternly states. Our Lord and Husband does not taunt and defraud us—beckoning us to Him, then cruelly refusing to come into spiritual union with us. He wants us to know Him intimately, and He longs to reveal Himself intimately to us, as we have just seen in John 14:21. He calls to even those of us who are "sleeping with the enemy" to arise, come to Him and take His hand in holy, eternal matrimony. In His embrace, we find cleansing, mercy, and grace. Just as He extended His arms on the cross, even now He opens wide His arms and bids us come to Him and receive Him as God's unspeakable gift. Christ offers to us His undeserved, unfathomable love.

Many choose to refuse His proposal.

But what about you?

Like the unrepentant criminal and the misled, "immoral majority" of humanity, are you so concerned for your own interests that you don't really care about the Lord and His interests? Instead of living dependently upon Him, eager to do only His will and bring joy to Him, does your life revolve around the question: "What's in it for *me?*"—just seeing how much you can get from Him and from others? Are you more interested in saving your life than in trustingly giving your life to the Lord Jesus to do with you as He pleases? Do you speak of Him, yet do not obey His commands?

Remember (as the Lord Jesus Himself has said in Matthew 7:21-23), not everyone who says to Him "Lord, Lord" will enter His eternal kingdom. It will not be those who merely proclaimed His lordship who will be saved from eternal death and hell, but those who lived in submission to Him as Lord, obeying Him diligently.

They who are truly His do not merely talk the walk. They also (and primarily) walk the talk. He will not be the Savior of any who will not accept and follow Him as Lord.

Hopefully, you relate more to the other criminal, the one whose attitude toward the Lord Jesus changed dramatically as he hung beside Him. Although he had lived in blatant rebellion against God, he finally came to his senses, willingly confessing that he was worthy of death for his anarchy. Convicted of his sin, he chose to turn from his stubborn hardness of heart and rebellious independence from God.

He saw that he needed the authority and rule of the Lord over his life. Recognizing Jesus Christ as King, this criminal chose to submit to Christ's rule fully and exclusively. In brokenness and desperation, he humbled himself, calling out to Jesus, realizing that the only way he would ever be able to enter Christ's kingdom would be through the Lord's abundant and undeserved mercy and kindness. And because the Lord is merciful and full of love and forgiveness, the man's sincere humility and repentance did not go unrewarded. Graciously, he was received by the Lord Jesus as one of His own who will forever be with Him.

Even in the final stages of such a torturously painful physical death, this man had probably never sensed such life, joy, and peace. In opening up his heart to the Spirit of God's testimony concerning Jesus Christ, the glorious reality and fulfillment of being granted a genuine relationship with the Living God surely must have flooded his being.

Know that his was no so-called "deathbed confession." If his sentence had suddenly been remitted and he had been removed from the cross before he died, I am certain that he would have been a committed and obedient follower and disciple of Jesus Christ.

What Is Your Choice?

As we have considered Jesus Christ's crucifixion, we have seen how nearly all responses to Him throughout the centuries, right down to this present time, were expressed by the different groups of people who witnessed his trial and death:

We looked at the pride of those who unjustly judged Him and condemned Him to die. We considered the indifference of those who have crowded God out of their lives for the pursuit of earthly things. We looked at the response of those who boasted in their earthly lineage, thereby forfeiting their right to partake of Christ's heavenly lineage. We noticed the wickedness and cruelty of the soldiers who put Him to death.

And then we considered the responses to Jesus Christ of those who were crucified on either side of Him. With practically his dying breath, one cursed and mocked Christ. The other, while at first also joining in the madness and cruelty of the crowd, chose to open his heart to the reality of Christ's claims as King of the heavenly kingdom.

Many that day were given the opportunity to receive or reject Christ. Apparently, only one of those we considered humbly turned from stubborn and damning rebellion to cast Himself on Jesus Christ's mercies and forgiveness. Only one believed that Christ was Who He had claimed to be—the rightful and soon to rule King of the heavenly Kingdom of God. The others could have sided with the repentant man, but they chose not to do so. No one but themselves could be blamed for their adamant refusal to turn to Jesus in genuine repentance, sincere sorrow for their sins, and deep humility.

What will *you* do with Jesus?

Will you align yourself with the noisy, reckless throng who rejected Him, either with open hostility or with bland indifference? [Remember that seeking for the approval of men can jeopardize our souls. If we live to please others, we will fail to please God.]

Do not think that religious pursuits will make you right with God. Recall that those who were most "religious" (in the sense that they observed many religious practices, studied the Word of God, and told others about God) were the very ones who hated Jesus Christ the most and labored most earnestly and eagerly for His death. Their many efforts and activities that they claimed were done in the name of God did not secure a relationship with Him. To the contrary, though they claimed to be God's chosen and beloved, in reality, because of their self-righteous independence they were His distant enemies. They had no inheritance in His kingdom.

Will you go against the downward pull of the polluted stream of this present age, or will you take the path of least resistance and thus be swept into a Godless eternity? Will you cling to your independence from God, remaining a "spiritual criminal and anarchist?" Or, will you join with the repentant thief, acknowledging your independence and rebellion against God and the rightful claims of King Jesus to rule and reign over you?

Before you are hasty with a decision to spurn Him and choose instead to be your own king and do your own thing, consider this: Jesus Christ did not have to die. He did what He did because He loves you and He wanted to please God Who also loves you so very much. In fact, so great is His love, He even sent His Son—Jesus the Messiah—to fully pay the price for humanity's rebellion—*your* rebellion—of independence from God. As Jesus says in John 3:16-17, "For God so greatly loved and dearly prized the world that He even gave His only begotten (unique) Son, so that whoever believes in Him (cleaves to Him, trusts Him, and relies on Him) shall not perish (come to destruction, be lost) but have eternal life. For God did not send His Son into the world in order to judge (to reject, to condemn, to pass sentence on) the world, but that the world might find salvation and be made safe and sound through Him."

Thanks be to God that Jesus' coming to earth to rescue us when it was impossible for us to do so on our own was a mission accomplished. His perfect, Divine life became the perfect, Divine sacrifice that will forever be sufficient to redeem for God everyone who will call on Him for deliverance and full salvation.

Yet, although the preceding is true, we must be certain to do as Paul urges us to do in Romans 11:22, "Behold therefore the goodness (kindness) and severity of God: severity toward those who have fallen, but goodness (kindness) to you—provided you continue in His grace and abide in His kindness; otherwise you too will be cut off (pruned away)."

We must not lose sight of the fact that the Day is coming when He will say, "I never knew you" to those who refused His offer of love and forgiveness. Nevertheless, there shall be those who will be able to stand before Him and ask, *"Lord, Remember Me?"* And they shall hear him respond with love and joy in His voice, "Oh yes, I remember you!"

He Did It For You

"**L**ord, remember Me..." the Lord Jesus was listening to the plea of His condemned crucifixion companion— a dying convict.

A marred, tainted sinner.

A castaway.

A reject of society.

A "loser" according to most people's standards. The majority of folks would consider him an unlikely candidate to receive a revelation from God.

Not so.

On the contrary, as 1 Corinthians 1:26-29 tells us, most followers of Jesus Christ are not thought of by others as wise, powerful, or rich when God calls them, neither are many of them of noble birth. James 2:5 reveals that God has chosen those who are poor in the eyes of the world to be rich in faith (which is spiritual perception and pursuit) and to inherit the kingdom He promised to those who love Him. God delights in lifting up the weak and lowly so that the strength and glory manifested in and through them will clearly be identified as His. He loves to work with a little and make it a lot. That way, no one will be able to brag in His presence. He will get all of the glory.

This doesn't mean that the rich, the powerful, the influential, and those who are well respected cannot enter God's kingdom. Unfortunately, however, most of those who "have it together" in this life according to the world's standards do not sincerely seek the Lord. Those in this present world who are considered "successful" apart from God usually grasp for things that are temporary and therefore remain separated from Him. The majority of them set their eyes and hearts on this present world, tragically sacrificing eternal rewards for temporal pleasures and pursuits— giving up things that will always last, they live for those which are fading fast.

Those who are hurting (like the repentant criminal who was crucified with the Lord Jesus) or who are unsatisfied in this present world tend to more readily recognize and acknowledge their need of the Lord than those who feel satisfied and at ease. They are also more often able and willing to comprehend and embrace the purpose for which Christ came to earth. The fact is, however, that whether we are poor or rich, "low-life" or respectable, influential or one of "the little people," all of us are in need of God and the life and purpose He offers us in His Son.

The Main Issue

Have you done things that you regret or not done things you wish you had? The main issue is not so much the things that we have or have not done, but whether we have accepted the Lord Jesus Christ as the rightful ruler of our lives. If not, we will often find ourselves embracing things we should not desire while neglecting or outright rejecting the things we should refuse. Will we stubbornly maintain a grasp on the *reins* of our lives instead of acknowledging and submitting to His right to *reign* over us?

He willingly suffered, bled, and died for everyone, including you. Now, what will be your response to the resurrected Christ of the cross?

Forget Mama's and Daddy's opinion on this one. It doesn't matter what your best friends or peer group thinks about this issue. If the whole world went to Hell and were cast into the Lake Of Fire, it wouldn't make it one degree cooler or more tolerable for you.

It is *your* choice.

Will you open your heart to Him and give to Him the reins of your life? Will you acknowledge that you no longer have the right to demand your own way, that He has the right to rule your life now? After all, He took our place in death. How can we do anything less than acknowledge that our lives are rightfully His? He bought us, as it were, with His very life and blood. Will you allow Jesus Christ to cover you with His forgiveness and fill you with His sweet, cleansing, and empowering Presence?

You can't earn this wonderful gift of divine love. He gives it freely to those who fully give themselves to Him. Give Him your all and He will be your All in all.

Have you ever acknowledged that you have lived in rebellion against God? You may or may not have committed terrible acts, but all of us have at times lived independently of God, choosing to depend upon our own efforts and the efforts of others.

All of us have fretted instead of trusting Him.

Lusted instead of loving.

Hated instead of forgiving.

We have taken pride in accomplishments that we were able to do only because of God's great and enabling love, mercy, and kindness.

Yet, all who will now turn from their own ways as they call on Jesus Christ to be their Lord and Savior have no reason to fear His return. He stretched out His arms, inviting sinful and fallen humanity to Himself. He died in humanity's place, securing pardon and freedom from condemnation for all who will receive the gift of life He offers.

Jesus Christ has paid the full price for our rebellion against God.

The work is done.

God's holiness and justice has been satisfied.

IT IS FINISHED!!!

Complete.

Fulfilled.

Lacking *nothing.*

The Lord has been raised from the dead.

And He, the coming Judge of all, is in love with you.

His resurrection life is available to whoever will receive Him, enabling us to live in consistent obedience to Him and unbroken fellowship and union with Himself and God the Father. And, bless His name(!), His blood and love are upon us with a ready, inexhaustible, and eternal cleansing for our sins.

The price has been paid.

Now, on us, His love is stayed...

He did it for all—for them, for us, for me.

*He Did It For **You.***

6

First Relationship, Then Fellowship

What if someone was told (or just convinced himself) that he belonged to a certain family even though, in actuality, he did not. Due to this deception, he began showing up for their family dinners and reunions, all the while considering others in the family his relatives.

He might really like the family members, the food they ate, the clothes they wore, the lifestyle they lived, and the homes in which they dwelled. He might even pick up some of the family's mannerisms, favorite phrases, and general tastes in music.

Nevertheless, none of these facts would procure a place in the family for him.

Even so, things might work out pretty good until the time for the dividing of the family inheritance. How distressing and disappointing it would be to then discover that he had no claim to the inheritance or any other privilege of family membership because he was not really a part of the family!

Similar to this self-proclaimed man, many today who are not God's children claim to be the heirs of God and members of His family. They fellowship with those who really do belong to His family, and, in many ways, they appear to be God's children. But they have never established relationship with the Lord through being born again. [John 3:7.] They have not turned from their own ways to follow the Lord and His ways and have not accepted what Jesus did for them on the cross and in the resurrection. Therefore, they do not have the ability to lay claim to the blessings and benefits that belong to those who are truly God's children.

Those seven Sons of Sceva we considered in the preceding chapter come to mind again. Having not received Jesus as Messiah and as their only hope of salvation, they were not united to Him by the Holy Spirit. Remember, John 8:44 points out that spiritually, Satan is the father of many people. Therefore, just because God is the Creator of all, He is not the Father of all. We become members of His family only through a spiritual rebirth.

Thus, because they had not experienced spiritual rebirth, spiritually they were not sons of God who were members of His family—the household of faith—and thus had no authority or right to use His name. The benefits that belong to God's family, like being able to cast out devils in Jesus' name, were not theirs to enjoy. Like the deluded fellow in our story who had no right to lay claim of the family's inheritance, they met with disappointment and disaster. They discovered that Jesus' name is not a magic wand.

To try to use the name of Jesus without first submitting to Him as our Lord and Savior is even more out of line than those deceptive people who try to accomplish things in life by posing as police officers when they are not. To do so would be considered fraudulent because the authority of police officers would not be theirs to claim. They would first have to become police officers to utilize rightfully the power and authority of the police.

Similarly, we must first become "born again" by the Spirit of God before we can rightfully claim to be members of God's household.

When Jesus spoke of being born again [John 3:5-7; 6:63], He was speaking of spiritual rebirth. [We will look at this more closely in the next chapter.] Our willful rebellion against God has caused us all to become dead towards Him, cut off from relationship and intimacy with Him. We all would remain separated from God forever without a sovereign work of His merciful "grace," which is "His undeserved favor, power, and influence to do His will."

Relationship With the Lord Is Initiated By the Lord

As a matter of fact, without such a work of mercy and grace on His part, we wouldn't even *desire* a relationship with Him. We are totally dependent on God if we truly desire to know Him. Our very salvation depends on our dependency on Jesus, for even our relationship *with* God must be initiated *by* God.

We see this in John 6:44 and 65, where our Lord revealed that no one can come to Him (and to God through Him) unless God has drawn them to Him—actually "enabled" them to do so. Thus, if we have any inclination towards a genuine relationship with the Living God, it is totally because the Lord is wooing us to Himself.

His Spirit works to convict us of sin, reveal Christ to us within our hearts, and woo us to submit fully to Him as our Lord. It is His Spirit Who reveals Christ to us, in us, and through us. He calls us to know Jesus intimately, love Him without reservation, and obey Him without hesitation.

Merely purposing to do good deeds and "staying out of trouble" will not save anyone and secure a relationship with Jesus, nor will "playing church." That is, relationship with God is not secured by just "cleaning-up our act" or getting our name on a membership roll. It is not accomplished by joining some well respected, deed-doing, philanthropic organization, or by going to a building or becoming a member of what many call "church." I say that they *call* it "church" because, in actuality, the church is made up of the true people of God, not the building in which they meet or some group or denomination they may join.

In short, the church is a living, vibrant *organism,* not a dead, static *organization.* Its structure and order is divine, not man-made. Although there is a perfect order and synchronicity to its life and function, God intended that it would be marked by the leading of His Holy spirit, not the rules, rituals, patterns, and plans of men. Their gatherings were not to be known for ritualistic forms dominated by a few professional clergy, but for a holy, joyful, spontaneous expression of the life of Jesus Christ in and through *each* of His people—from the least to the greatest.

Thus, we see that true *Christ*ianity is not the *church*ianity that most of the world has seen.

Know also that relationship and fellowship with God are not accomplished by some "easy-believism" which is contrary to true believing in the Biblical sense of the word. We must have right hearts, not just right words. For example, someone may teach a parrot to quote Scriptures, claim promises, sing hymns, and say all sorts of "right things," but that would not mean that the parrot was saved. Similarly, salvation hinges on more than merely saying or believing the right things or acknowledging that something is true. Even the demons "believe" and "parrot" in this sense.

The "Believing" of Demons

In Scripture passages such as Matthew 8:28-29 and Luke 4:41, we discover that even demons believe some correct facts about God and His Son. Some, like those mentioned in these and other verses such as Mark 1:24, 5:7, and Luke 8:28, are even willing to publicly acknowledge Who Jesus is! James 2:19 also reveals that even demons believe that there is one God (and they actually tremble at this thought!). However, in spite of their even sometimes-religious displays, the demons are not saved. Furthermore, their outward show of praise of the Lord Jesus as He walked in the earth was refused by Him because it was not genuine—it did not come from hearts desirous of nor even capable of brokenness and repentance.

For, even though they had once known and served God as holy angels, the damned fate of demons was sealed ages ago when they turned their backs on Him, deliberately choosing darkness and death over light and life, and Satan's lies in place of God's truth. They became and will forever be unholy angels with heads full of knowledge *about* light, life, and truth, but hearts totally hardened against the truth that are full of darkness, death, and lies.

From Full Of Light To Full of Darkness

Have you ever stared at a light bulb or briefly looked at the sun, then immediately looked away? Everything seems so dark. You can't see anything for a while. Similarly, when The Truth is known and rejected, in its place comes a darkness that is far greater than would have been there had the Truth never been known. [See Matthew 12:41-45; Luke 11:24-26, 49-51; 2 Peter 2:20-21.] This is what happened to the "fallen" angels. Having turned their backs on God Who is light, these rebellious creatures plunged themselves into total, inconceivable spiritual darkness.

Similar to demons, many people walk through life with much head knowledge and mental information but with no heart experience and spiritual transformation. They know many facts about Jesus Christ and His kingdom, but they do not choose to submit to Him as Lord and really come to know Him. This does not impress Him.

Spouting out Scripture from a full head but an empty heart (or a heart full of love for other things rather than for the Spirit of Jesus Christ) is an unacceptable confession to the Lord. We must possess what we profess.

Our *profession* lacks *possession* if we have not truly turned from our selfish desires to pursue the Lord and His desires. Bended knees do not necessarily indicate a bended heart. Remember the words of our Lord Jesus in Matthew 7:21, "Not everyone who *says* to me 'Lord, Lord,' will enter the kingdom of Heaven, but only He who *does* the will of My Father Who is in Heaven."

If we are to have a better reward than the demons, if we would bring praise and honor to God that He accepts, and if we desire to enjoy eternal life with Him rather than eternal torment apart from Him, we had better do more than merely commit some facts *about* the Living God to memory. Also, we are to commit everything we have and are *to* Him, fully. Then, rather than merely having informed minds, we will also have transformed hearts. The result will be changed, selfless, holy lives.

If we desire fellowship with God, we must first establish a relationship with Him—*First Relationship, **Then** Fellowship.*

———————————

Let's now consider the requirements that must be satisfied in order for us to have with God this relationship and fellowship of which we speak…

There are requirements we must satisfy for us to be able to really know the Lord…

7

The Relationship's Requirements
After The Application Of The Law Of God—Conviction

Before we can become God's children, we must be brought to a state of mind and heart where we are convicted of rebelling—that is, sinning—against the only God Who is indescribably holy—totally unmarred by sin and its proud, selfish self-absorption. Conviction occurs when the Holy Spirit presses the requirements of the Law upon our hearts. He does this by pressing upon our consciences and minds the godly standards of the Scriptures. This in turn brings us to the realization that we measure-up nowhere near to God's standards of holiness and love.

Without the dealings of the Holy Spirit within us and the revealing work of the Scriptures, we'd just settle for smugly and with prejudice comparing ourselves with one another. This is the reason the Law of God in the Old Testament is so vital to us since, as Romans 7:7 tells us, without the Law we would not even have a knowledge of what sin is.

It is true that having knowledge of the Law and a sincere and earnest attempt to fulfill it cannot save us. But God uses the Law to convince and convict us of our sin in preparation for us to receive Jesus Christ as our Lord and Savior.

When we are saved, the Spirit of God first brings us to the recognition that we are rebellious anarchists against the Lord God. Our hearts are smitten as we learn of His holiness and our lack of it. He shows us that we are sinners because we have offended Him—the holy God—by going our own way, thereby rejecting Him and His ways. Because of the rebellion of our hearts, we deserve death, even damnation in The Lake Of Fire that will forever torment those who chose in this life to remain in prideful, rebellious independence away from God.

The purposes of these sobering revelations from God (whether we consciously are aware of all of them when they are taking place or not) is not to just make us feel bad. Rather, God is pursuing us through our hearts. It is in our spirits—our hearts—where He desires to reside within us and spread His kingdom. So, before He can reign within us, He must bring us to the place where are willing to depose every other false god in our hearts. Strongholds of rebellion within us must be destroyed so that He can "set up house" within us. For us to be willing to give to God our clinging to self-rule, He must bring us to the end of ourselves. This is one reason for the convicting work of the Holy Spirit, for, when our hearts become convicted of sin, they can then become broken of their pride and self-sufficiency.

At this point at the onset of our spiritual trek toward God and His eternal kingdom, if we are honest with Him and ourselves we will acknowledge that we are helplessly lost apart from His mercies. As Ephesians 2:12 reveals, there is no hope outside of Him. We are in need of the Savior to deliver us from the tyranny of sin, the awful torments of conscience, and the fear and penalty of hell and ultimate damnation in The Lake Of Fire.

When we become convinced of our sinful condition and the speedily approaching Judgment, the resulting brokenness, sorrow, and even fear of God's anger and retributions against sinners can be devastating to us. This miserable, tormented state of being is actually a taste of damnation itself.

But, as horrible and traumatic as such a condition is it is actually a tremendous blessing because it is almost always instrumental in bringing us to the end of ourselves and our stinking, self-sufficient pride. And, in order to prepare us for living forever with God, it is better to figuratively "go through some Hell" now, so to speak, than to literally be cast into Hell forever, there to suffer eternal torment, cutoff from Him.

Seeing the reality of our need to be saved from ourselves and the tormenting reality of these things leads us to call on God for His mercy. Thank God that He is not only holy, but also merciful and full of forgiving love. It is not His desire for us to go through life and face death and the Judgment apart from being right with Him.

After Conviction–Repentance

After conviction, the Holy Spirit leads us through the door of repentance. The pathway of repentance is the only road that leads to the highway of holiness and to genuinely experiencing God through salvation and eternal life.

In their presentation of the Gospel, many have overlooked the absolute necessity of repentance. This, however, does not change the fact that both John the Baptist and the Lord Jesus Himself declared repentance as the first prerequisite we must embrace if we are to have relationship with God and entrance into His Kingdom. In Matthew 3:1 and 2, we read the heart of this message that John the baptizer declared to his generation: "Repent, for the kingdom of Heaven is at hand." And the first we hear of Jesus' preaching, we read: "...Jesus came to Galilee, preaching the Gospel of the Kingdom of God, and saying, 'The time is fulfilled, and the kingdom of God is at hand. Repent, and believe in the Gospel.' " [Mark 1:14b-15; also see Matthew 5:17.]

So we see that repentance is one of the fundamental changes that we *must* have in order to enter the Kingdom of God (we shall consider "believing" in a moment). Repentance literally means, "to change our minds." In genuine repentance, our focus, perspectives, pursuits, and whole outlook on life change. We turn from going one direction to go the opposite way. From following our own selfish plans, purposes, and pursuits, we choose to turn and follow the Lord.

Without repentance, we are not ready to believe the Gospel and enter into an intimate relationship with the Lord Jesus. When we repent, we give the right to rule our lives to Jesus Christ. We are then in a condition of mind and heart to receive the gift of a new life built on forgiveness from God, dependency on God, and friendship and fellowship with Him.

In short: N-o repentance—no relationship. K-n-o-w repentance— know relationship.

Repentance, Like Marriage, Is A Turning To, Not Just A Turning From

The Lord Jesus has chosen us to be a part of His life and dreams, just as a loving husband does for his beloved bride. As our Husband from Heaven, He desires that He alone be the darling and consuming passion of our hearts. All who are a part of the bride of Christ are to forsake all other "loves" that we might be totally His, following Him in loving, non-swerving devotion. This includes forsaking any egocentric love of self that causes us to be proud, self-sufficient, and in pursuit of self-centered desires instead of being in love with God and others, desirous to do only His will.

In true repentance, the Lord isn't just added to the loves of our hearts; He becomes *the* love of our hearts. As one familiar saying goes, "If Jesus is not Lord *of* all, then He's not your Lord *at* all."

We are to die to everything but Him. He, in turn, will place everything else in our lives in its proper place and perspective. We just must continue to follow Him.

In marriage, a man and a woman choose to turn from their old ways—their lifestyles of being single—so that they can embark on a totally new way of living and being. In a sense, they "repent" of their singleness—that is, they turn *from* it. But even more importantly, they turn *to* one another in marriage. This is a wonderful analogy of what takes place in repentant hearts. Their primary focus is not on *from* what they are turning, but rather, *to* Whom they are turning. The emphasis is not primarily on the past and what we have done, but on the future and fulfilling what we were created (and recreated) to do.

Usually, people think repentance is feeling bad about past wrongs, going through a long, drawn out process of being filled with guilt-ridden fears and remorse, crying many tears, and experiencing a terrible, difficult time of painful introspection and self-loathing. Certainly, many (probably most) people have experienced all of these things and even more as they repented.

However, there may or may not be much pain and remorse as we "die" to our own ways. The main issue in repentance is not so much about feeling bad regarding things we've done (or not done) as it is in turning from our own pursuits to wholeheartedly embrace the Lord and His ways. It involves desiring to obey Him in every area from this moment forward and developing an intimate relationship with Him.

Inward Work Leads To Outward Evidences

Whether we feel much emotion or absolutely none at all does not determine if we have genuinely repented or not. What we feel is not the proof of genuine repentance. Rather, it's what we do (as well as cease from doing). Living righteously and doing deeds of kindness that are born of the Spirit of God will follow repentance as surely as crops follow rain. Righteous acts are the genuine fruits of repentance. Ephesians 2:10 refers to them as "good works which God prepared beforehand that we should walk in them."

These good works are the inevitable, outward, overt evidences of an inward, covert transformation of character. For, as we truly repent, the Lord takes up residence within us and His Spirit begins to develop His character qualities in our hearts. As we have previously mentioned, these are listed in Galatians 5:22-23 and are called "the fruit of the Spirit." They are "love, joy, peace, patience (longsuffering), kindness (gentleness), goodness, faithfulness, gentleness (meekness), and self-control."

Notice, these qualities are the fruit of the Spirit—not of ourselves. I've never seen a tree "grunting and groaning" in an attempt to produce fruit. It grows as it abides in good soil, getting adequate water, nutrients, and sunshine. Similarly, we cannot produce fruit by trying harder. As branches attached to Jesus the Vine [see John 15:1-8], we will produce spiritual fruit only as we remain vitally united to Him through our obedience to Him. Similarly, 2 Peter 3:18 tells us to "grow in grace," that is, we are to be totally dependent on God's unmerited favor, power, and influence.

The secret of growth in Christ is to abide in Him—listening to Him and obeying His Word. Then, as Isaiah 61:3 tells us, we will be "...trees of righteousness, the planting of the Lord, that He may be glorified." We will surely "bear fruit" if we rest in the "soil" of God's mercy and grace found in Jesus Christ. We must have the "roots" of our beings go down deeply into Him [Colossians 2:7], receive washing and renewal through the "water" of God's Word [Ephesians 5:26], and bask in the healing, strengthening beams of the "*Son* of God" Who is also the "*Sun* of Righteousness" spoken of in Malachi 4:2.

As we have previously pointed out, our growth *in* Christ is all *of* Christ—our responsibility is to respond to *His* ability, and even this is a gift of God's grace. From start to finish, salvation is not something we can earn or merit. It is a gift from God that we receive by receiving Jesus Christ, the One The Revelation 1:8; 22:12 and Hebrews 12:2 refer to as "the A and the Z," "the Author and the Finisher, the Founder and the Perfecter of our faith."

After Repentance—Believing

Although we may be convicted of sin and sincerely repent and turn toward the Lord instead of run from Him, the miracle of salvation is not yet complete. Having been convicted and having repented, the next step is that we must believe what God has said concerning the salvation He has provided in His crucified and risen Son, clinging to Him as our only hope. At this time, the Holy Spirit strives with us to cast ourselves unreservedly on the Lord's mercies and believe in His promise of salvation to those who come to Him on His terms. And His terms are clear...

There is only one way of escape from certain, eternal terror and destruction: We must submit to Jesus the Christ as our only Lord, acknowledging that He is the One sent from God to die in our place for our rebellion. We must also confess that He fully paid the penalty for sin and God raised Him from the dead.

Most assuredly, we are to "believe on the Lord Jesus Christ" to be saved, just as Acts 16:31 tells us, but this does not mean just to believe facts about Him. Remember, in the previous chapter we saw that even demons believe some correct facts about the Lord, but they are, nonetheless, hopelessly lost. Believing that leads to salvation entails cleaving to and relying totally on the Lord Jesus Himself as our only hope and very life, willingly submitting to Him as our sovereign Lord, and accepting His gift of everlasting life with God secured through His finished work for us on the cross and in His resurrection. True believing that leads to salvation requires us to know and love the Lord Jesus *Himself,* not just things *about* Him.

Therefore, to repent and believe on the Lord Jesus Christ, we must first turn from our own pursuits, selfish ambitions, lusts, loves, and concepts. Then, we are to totally and unreservedly pursue Him through our loving obedience and passionate devotion to Him. We are to live to please *Him* (not ourselves) and fulfill His will, not our own. One benefit, however, of yielding fully to Jesus and following Him consistently is the fact that doing His will instead of our own will is the deepest of joys to hearts that have been submitted to Him and transformed by His Spirit. To serve Him is to satisfy the deepest needs and longings of a genuine disciple's "reborn" heart.

Rebirth

If we see and "believe" these things (embracing the truth about ourselves, the Lord Jesus, and the gift of life that He offers us in Himself); if we turn from our old lives of independence from God so that we can lay hold of the Lord Jesus to be our very Life, then the Spirit of God will cause us to be "born from above." In John 3:3 and 5, the Lord Jesus referred to it as being "born again," or being born "of the Spirit." This spiritual rebirth enables us to perceive and pursue the Kingdom of God. For, unless we are born again in our spirits, we cannot "see" nor experience the Kingdom of God [John 3:3.] We might know many facts about the Lord and His kingdom before becoming born again, but we will not be able spiritually to perceive Him and the things that He is doing.

Being born again is similar to natural birth in that, when we are born again, God gives us spiritual eyes and ears, so to speak. These enable us to perceive what is going on in the supernatural realm of His eternal, unseen kingdom just as physical eyes and ears equip us to perceive what is going on in the natural, temporal, visible realm.

The rebirth experience equips us with the ability to recognize and receive revelation from God's Spirit. Through Him, we are able to perceive God's supernatural hand in our everyday lives.

This rebirth experience involves the forgiveness of our sins, the cleansing of our spirits, and the actual joining of our spirits with the Spirit of the Lord. [1 Corinthians 6:17.] Then, as we choose to follow the inclinations of the new life within us (*His* very life), we are empowered by His holy, indwelling Presence to be able to live according to God's standards.

For Jesus Christ is not just our only hope of escaping the Law's demands for justice. He also is the only One Who can enable us to live up to the holy standards of the Law of total conformity to God's will and ways. He does this by sending His Spirit to dwell in those who receive, love, and obey Him. Then, from within, He grants power that has overcome sin.

Salvation—More Than Fire Insurance

Many people, when they think of salvation, imagine it to be mainly a "saving *from* Hell" that we might "go *to* Heaven." Salvation is more than just being saved *from* self, sin, and Hell. It primarily refers to being saved *for* God, holiness, and Heaven.

God's ultimate intent in saving sinners is to establish and enjoy an ongoing, ever-developing relationship with them, revealing Himself *to* them, then *in* them, then *through* them. We read of this unfolding revelation of Jesus in the apostle Paul's life in Galatians 1:11 and in verses 15-16.

The Lord's plan is to save us *from* both sin and Hell *for* Himself and His eternal purposes.

Eternal Life

Once we are saved, we are given eternal life. Just as our salvation is more a being saved *for* God rather than merely being saved *from* Hell, the real crux of eternal life is more than simply "living forever." While it is true that the people of God will enjoy ceaseless existence, this is not the central focus of eternal life. In actuality, every child of God does not readily experience eternal life...

For example, consider 1 Timothy 6:12. Paul is encouraging Timothy to lay hold of the eternal life to which he is summoned. Timothy was a devout and steadfast believer in the Lord Jesus Christ and a leader in the Church. If eternal life was something automatically experienced in fullness by being one of God's children, Paul would not have counseled Timothy to lay hold of it, for Timothy was certainly a child of God.

So, what is eternal life? It is an intimate, ongoing relationship and fellowship with the only true God and His Son—Jesus Christ. We learn this directly from the lips of Jesus in His prayer recorded in the seventeenth chapter of John. In verse three, our Lord prayed, "And this is eternal life: [it means] to know (to perceive, recognize, become acquainted with and understand) You, the only true and real God and [likewise] to know Him, Jesus [as the] Christ, the Anointed One, the Messiah, Whom You have sent." This is why Paul instructed Timothy to lay hold of it. Paul knew that just because Timothy belonged to God did not necessarily mean that he was growing more deeply acquainted with the Lord and coming to more intimately know the Lord Himself instead of just things about Him.

Furthermore, salvation is not just something the Lord gives us apart from Himself. *He* is salvation. Consider the name of the Son of God—"Jesus." His name is a transliteration of the Hebrew "Joshua," meaning, "Jehovah is salvation." [From Vine's Expository Dictionary.] Psalm 27:1; 38:22; 62:2, 6; 118:14; and Isaiah 12:2 are Scripture passages that refer to God Himself being salvation.

We see that eternal life and salvation are not just things that the Lord gives us apart from Himself. They are a part of His Person and of the intimate union and fellowship with Him to which He is calling us. All of God's blessings and gifts to us are in His Son. They are received and experienced only to the degree that we know *Him*.

Therefore, if we are to have relationship with God, we must accept His gift of life in His Son. Only through Him can we satisfy *The Relationship's Requirements.*

8

The Coat And The Pot

The Coat

Once upon a time, there was a kingdom full of joy and peace. Everywhere there was singing and rejoicing, and people and even the animals all got along with one another.

One day, however, a cruel and evil prince—the founder of the dark, forbidden arts—deceived the wife of the peoples' leader and convinced her to do as he said. She in turn persuaded her husband to join her in her folly. The result was the removal of an invisible aura of protection around them, and the evil prince brought a curse on the land and on everyone in it. The curse had to do with a magical coat that was placed on each person in the land and would be placed on all of his or her unborn children throughout the ages.

The coat covered them completely and had much elasticity. It even stretched as they grew, continuing to cover them. After awhile, they grew accustomed to constantly wearing it, so much so, they become convinced that wearing it all the time was just the way things are supposed to be. They even got to where they thought that the cumbersome, bothersome coat was actually a part of them.

This coat represents the condition of sin into which all of us are born and is produced by our aberrant, righteousness-deficient, "spiritual genetic code."

In the pockets of this "coat" known as "sin," we stuff different things known as "sins." These are the selfish actions and attitudes that are produced because of the existence of sin. Without the coat, there would be no place to store the things we place in its pockets—without the presence of sin within us, there would not be the existence of sins in our lives.

Some coats are big. Some are small. Some stand out in a crowd. Others are rather plain and unassuming.

The state of rebellion towards God and His ways is obvious in some people, clearly seen by everyone, while in others, their attitude of anarchy toward God is not evident at all by people. Others will not perceive their true, inner condition until the Day of Judgment, as 1 Timothy 5:24 declares.

Sin can even appear to be reasonable, appealing, and very well refined. It may be evidenced by an attitude of disinterested apathy and nonchalance towards God. Or, it may express itself in blatant defiance. Or, it may possibly cloak itself in religious zeal that is taken up with activities and rituals *about* God, yet lacks His love and wisdom that come as a result of focus *on* God Himself.

Observing religious rituals does not make anyone holy. Having a religion *about* God is not the same as having a relationship *with* Him. And just because someone may say they are part of "the religious right" does not make them right at all. After all, many hearts bound in the grip of sin love to be perceived as very religious. Gaudy displays of outward shows of supposed devotion and affection for the Lord and His ways are substituted for sincere hunger and love for God and a desire to do only His will. However, the true nature and presence of sin is revealed by the lack of genuine dependency on Him.

On the contrary (though often hidden beneath a religious front and seeming piety), sin's most distinctive characteristics are: 1) living independently of God, 2) pride, and 3) self-reliance. These attitudes and strongholds of mind and heart prevent many from depending exclusively on Him and really coming to know Him.

Self-Sufficiency Strengthens Sin

No amount of self-effort will ever be able to remove this sorry coat of sin even though it might stink, look gaudy, and greatly hamper our ability to function as we desire. However, it can only be removed by God Himself.

Nevertheless, through much self-discipline and religious commitment, some almost seem to rid themselves entirely of the things in the pockets—that is, the sins. Many of them choose to live in seclusion, cutoff from others. A few even fervently embrace a lifestyle of attempted humility, extreme self-deprivation, and self-deprecation. Some will beat themselves bloody with whips whenever they feel that they have disappointed the Lord, or because of a sadly misguided concept of trying to bring their flesh under subjection to their spirits, presuming that they are showing the flesh who's boss.

But only God's sin-forgiving, life-giving, overcoming, resurrection power found in Jesus Christ His Son can conquer our flesh and its lusts. All efforts to control the flesh and curb its appetites through the power of the flesh only strengthen the flesh. We see this in Colossians 2:20-23, where we read: "If then you have died with Christ to material ways of looking at things and have escaped from the world's crude and elemental notions and teachings of externalism, why do you live as if you still belong to the world?— Why do you submit to rules and regulations such as, 'Do not handle this; do not taste that; do not even touch them,' referring to things all of which perish with being used. To do this is to follow human precepts and doctrines. Such [practices] have indeed the outward appearance [that popularly passes] for wisdom, in promoting self-imposed rigor of devotion and delight in self-humiliation and severity of discipline of the body, but they are of no value in checking the indulgence of the flesh. Instead, they do not honor God but serve only to indulge the flesh."

Nevertheless, many boast that they have fewer things in their pockets than most—they claim they do not indulge in the pleasures of sin as readily as most do. Yes, there are those who have a much better than average moral code and character and appear to be more together than others. Their "coat" seems to be so pretty and in so much better shape than most other coats. Because their coat is cleaner than nearly everyone else's and the pockets aren't nearly as full, its wearers usually are very proud and self-confident. "I'm not as bad as most people," they boast. "Just look at me—I've got my life pretty much together."

However, those who have this attitude usually wear the heaviest, most encumbering and smelliest coats of all. [Unfortunately, we can become so accustomed to our environment that we do not smell its (or *our*) offensive odors anymore.] Instead of them having a coat that is better than others, it is the one that God hates the most (people despise it, also).

After all, who enjoys the smell of filth, decay, and rottenness? And pride, self-reliance, and human effort apart from obedience to and dependency on God are a stench to God worse than putrefying garbage is to us. These conditions of mind and heart also only strengthen the hold of the self-ruled independence of sin in our lives and deepens our involvement in The Rebellion.

Therefore, no amount of self-effort to cleanup our act, nor any amount of comparing ourselves with others in the hope of making ourselves look good and feel better, will result in making us pleasing to God. On the contrary, rather than gross and overt acts of immorality, many times the enemy uses self-effort, self-sufficiency, and self-dependency as his "appealing" and socially acceptable—yet damning—substitutes for submission to God.

To please the Lord, we must cease from our own labors and enter into the rest into which He has entered, spoken of in Hebrews 4:1-11. In fact, Jesus Christ Himself is our rest, and we will experience Him as such if we will allow Him to accomplish His intents in and through us. He will do all of this, even removing the "coat" and its weighty cargo, but only if we accept His terms: First, we must recognize and acknowledge our need and desire to have the "coat" removed—desiring Him to set us free from sin and its manifestations (sins). Secondly, we must be willing to truly turn to God, which includes being willing to discard our "coat"—life of independence from Him and His ways.

Beware Of Unbelief, Believer

As we truly realize that sin is independence from God and not just outwardly wicked activities brings us to the sobering conclusion that even many followers of Jesus Christ sin (often and to a great degree) by choosing to turn from a continuing dependence on God. Such is the essence of unbelief, and, concerning it, we are told in Hebrews 3:12, "Beware, brethren, lest there be in any on you an evil heart of unbelief which refuses to cleave to, trust in, and rely on the living God—leading you to turn away and desert or stand aloof from Him."

Unbelief is not marked so much by a disbelieving state of mind and heart that denies the existence of God. Rather, it is evidenced by a detached indifference to Him or a lack of dependency on Him.

So, we see that disbelief is more often at work in those who are not God's children, whereas unbelief is more often a threat to those who are His.

To move in unbelief is to cease moving in the Spirit, for unbelief leads to a fruitless, empty, self-initiated, self-sustaining, wearying walk of self-righteousness (which is not true "righteousness" at all). In Galatians 3:1-18, Paul rebuked the Galatians for this, reminding them that in order to fully mature spiritually, we must abide in a place of dependency on God—a simple, non-polluted walk of purity and faith.

Linen, Wool, Sweating, B.O. And Purity

We need to remember the message of Jesus to us in John 15:5—apart from Him we can do nothing. We must stay aware of the fact that the Lord does not want us to work up a sweat in our service to Him.

Are you aware of the Lord's instruction regarding priests in Ezekiel 44: 17-18, and Exodus 28:39? They were to wear linen garments against their skin, not wool, because the Lord did not want them to wear anything that would make them sweat. Flesh that is sweating causes B.O.—it stinks! In the natural as well as the spiritual realm, the smell of sweaty, stinking flesh is nauseating. The references in Scripture regarding the sweatless garments to be worn by the priests symbolize God's disgust for independent, selfish sin and His intolerance of it. As His New Covenant priests [1 Peter 2:9; The Revelation 1:6; 5:10; and 20:6], we are to abide in Him and His rest without the least bit of foolish, futile, fleshly efforts in an attempt to accomplish His will without depending on His Holy Spirit and following His leading.

The Lord wants our humanity—our flesh—to be clothed with His righteousness and ability found only in His Son, not the heavy, sweat causing "coat" of sin and its religious endeavors. No amount of fleshly, human effort, program, or ingenuity will be allowed to enter into our life in God. It would only sour and spoil things.

Notice, too, in these analogies of both the coat and priests' clothing, that because of the garments, our flesh is not exposed. This signifies that the Lord Jesus is the One to be seen as we cover the nakedness of our own fleshly ways with Him. As we read in Romans 13:14, "...clothe yourself with the Lord Jesus Christ, the Messiah, and make no provision for [indulging] the flesh—put a stop to thinking about the evil cravings of your physical nature—to [gratify its] desires (lusts)." As we do this and walk in obedience to Him, He is seen and revealed instead of us, and He rightfully receives all the glory.

The requirement of God that for the priests to wear linen turbans portrays that the peace and purity of the Lord is to reign over our thought-life. Pants cover our genital area, the parts of our body needed for reproduction. The requirement of the priests to wear linen pants signify that the pure and peaceful leading of the Lord is to be the source of all that comes forth from us, not the striving and energy of our flesh. All things pertaining to us must be born of His holy seed, not the loins or womb of our human reasonings, strengths, and abilities. Our human ingenuity, efforts, strength, and fallen life are to be abandoned so that we can participate in His thoughts and His creation of new, spiritual life. We are to be covered with Jesus Christ as well as be vessels used by the Spirit of God to reveal Him.

In His love, He has warned us all to be done with the coat of sin and the things with which we love to load it down. All who choose to continue living wrapped in the gripping coat of the sinful rebellion will stand under the wrath of God and will surely be destroyed along with it if they don't cast it off and flee from it.

The Pot

Similarly, picture a pot that each of us has been holding since conception. On our own, we cannot get rid of it, and most don't even want to. Furthermore, everyone is convinced that the pot is part of their body—they feel that the pot is there because that's the way that it's supposed to be.

We place various things such as spoons and other utensils into this pot. Most of us place many spoons in the pot, others place only several, and a few of us seem to be able to rid the pot completely of any spoons.

The condition of sin that we have discussed is represented be the pot. The spoons and other utensils represent the sins that exist because of sin.

Some pots are shiny. Some are not. Some are exciting and bright to look at. Others are not very interesting at all. Some people love to show their pot to others, while some choose to try to convince others that they don't even have one. Some parade around with their pot on their heads. Still others love to sit on their pots. Others use their pots and spoons to hurt others, hitting anyone who gets in their way or even within their reach.

There are those who use their pots to feed others, or to dip water out of a well for another. But remember, the pot represents sin, so, even though the deeds performed appear to be noble, the motivation and energy to do these "good deeds" does not come from the Lord. Instead, they come from the human heart—fallen, yet still capable of seemingly sublime expressions of kindness and selflessness that are actually self-aggrandizement in disguise.

This pot of sin represents independence from God is always unacceptable to Him, and anything "cooked" in this pot (any motive, thought, or deed that does not come from total submission to God) is also intolerable to Him—He cannot "stomach" anything that is prepared in this pot. Remember, as Isaiah 64:6 says, "...we are all like an unclean thing, and all our righteous acts" (or, "our righteousness") "are like filthy rags." No matter how noble the pot and its actions may seem to be, as long as we are sitting on the throne of our lives, all of the so-called "good" we may think we are doing is unacceptable to the Lord because its source of inspiration and empowerment is rooted in pride and rebellious independence from God.

Those who boast that their pots are not as ugly or as full of stuff as others' pots are really in a worse shape than those whose pots are filthy and full of stuff (this "stuff" represents wickedness, evil longings and sinful attitudes). As we have previously seen, pride and self-sufficiency are more deplorable and disgusting to God than any blatant wickedness of the flesh.

Thank God, He has provided a way of escape from the control and dominion of sin as well as His judgments against it and its manifestations. Jesus Christ, our crucified and risen sin bearer [Isaiah 53:11], has become our deliverance and our salvation. On our behalf, He took upon Himself the terrifying and eternal judgments of God against sin and the sins it causes.

However, when the Lord confronts us with an offer to receive the gift of eternal life in Christ Jesus His Son, we cannot do so if our hands are grasping any other thing. We must come to the Lord empty-handed, hungry, and in complete honesty, holding nothing back. There can be no attempt to hide anything from Him. Instead, we readily need to acknowledge our need of Him as well as our emptiness and utter impoverishment apart from His kind, undeserved intervention.

Only if we would obey God's command to lay aside the "coat" of independent self can we be clothed with Jesus Christ. And our head should be crowned with the helmet of salvation, not the "pot" of sin. Neither should we "cover our rears" with a "pot." Rather, the glory of the Lord is to be our "rear" guard.

As we were once in sin, so we can now be in Christ. Once attached to "the coat" or "the pot" (that is, to "sin"), we can now be united with Christ. For, if we will listen to His Holy Spirit, allowing Him to bring us to complete submission to the Lordship of Jesus, then God will take off of us the coat of sin and clothe us with His Son, the Lord Jesus Christ. He will take the pot away, replacing it with His Word—the sword of the Spirit—and His sweet Presence.

God's Primary Intent

We need to realize that God's primary intent is for us constantly to have our attention focused on His Son, not on whether we can rid ourselves of sin and its manifestations. On our own, we surely cannot. In fact, as we have seen, our own attempts to rid ourselves of sin and its manifestations only strengthens sin's hold on us. This occurs because the very act of trying to live apart from total dependency on the Son of God is an act of supreme anarchy and rebellion towards God. Regardless of how good such an action might seem to be, it is only one of God defying, flesh deifying religion.

However, the Lord Jesus is more than able to set us free from the power of sin and the sins that flow from it. Defeat by sin can give way to the glorious reality of living through the power of the Holy Spirit of the Lord Jesus Christ and His victorious, resurrection life. [Romans 13:11-14; Ephesians 4:17-25; Colossians 3:1-10.]

A Putting Off And A Putting On

By our choice, we put off the old—independent pride and its resultant sinful habits (the "coat" and the "pot")—and put on the new—Jesus Christ and His ways. As we choose to believe the established fact that Jesus' victory is ours to experience (and not just talk about), and as we turn from all that would try to distract us from focusing and depending on Jesus Christ, we shall experience His immeasurable and unsurpassed resurrection power working in and through us. This will help to transform us, others, and often, our circumstances, too. By being in love with Him and the eternal things of His kingdom, we will be set free from the demands and power of this present world. As we focus on Him and His desires, He will set us free from the grip and tyranny of sin. We will find ourselves having both the desire and the ability to turn from sin and fully accomplish God's will. Only as we abide in Him—living each day with our hearts in love with Him—will we be able to overcome all the works of the devil, which are sin and the sins it produces. [See Romans 6:11-12; Hebrews 12:1-3; 2 Thessalonians 3:3; 1 Thessalonians 3:13; 5:23-24; Romans 16:20; 1 John 3:4-8.]

We don't need to try to get the uncleanable coat clean. We need not try to polish the unpolishable pot. If we will let Him, Jesus Christ will remove them from our lives, replacing them with love for Himself and His ways. Then, we shall experience the reality of moral and spiritual freedom and be completely done with *The Coat And The Pot.*

9

The King's Day Of Reckoning, And The Price of Freedom

The king had had enough. With kindness and generosity, he had sustained his subjects. He loved them dearly, and had expressed the extent of his love by sending his heir and only son into a furious war against an unfathomably evil tyrant and his kingdom of bondage, despair, and terror. This sadist tortured his prisoners, mercilessly binding them, blinding them, and destroying their hearing.

By laying down his own life, the good king's son had made the ultimate sacrifice. Thereby, he freed his father's people from the slavery that they had willingly embraced and had even empowered through their own pride, selfishness, and rebellious hearts. Yet, even with this display of love, most of the king's subjects refused to be thankful. They even scorned and mocked his son.

But their ignoring Him finally came to an end...

The king had long ago appointed a day when he would reward those who devotedly loved Him and destroy those who refused to accept his right to rule. How it grieved him to think of bringing judgment on the rebels. How often he had reached out to them, nurtured them, and helped them through difficult times. They would not have even survived were it not for his undeserved mercy and kindness, which was largely unappreciated or even unnoticed.

But the day of reckoning came...

Yet, not without warning, for the king had often sent messengers to his people to warn them that this day would come. Repeatedly, He had earnestly warned them to be prepared for it by choosing to submit to his rule, proving their loyalty by their obedience to Him.

Still, most were not ready for this day of days. Therefore, they awaited their turn before the king in his "Hall of Justice" with a sense of dread and ever increasing terror. For them, it was too late.

But there were also those who were ready. Those who had gladly accepted the king as their king—those who had willingly obeyed him because they loved him—was assured of reward beyond comprehension. Their devotion to the king, while at times extremely difficult and even costly, proved to be the best thing that they could have chosen. Not only did it bring them peace and joy during the time of preparation, but now that the day of reckoning had come, it proved to be the key to their future and to receiving treasures beyond measure.

Life is much like this tragic and triumphant story. God loves us so much that He sent His Son to take our punishment for our rebellion against Him (which we have so willingly embraced). Satan—the head of the regime at the heart of The Rebellion—is certainly the most terrible of tyrants and the most hard and cruel of taskmasters. "Sin" (as this rebellion is called) is certainly blinding, causing Satan's prisoners to be spiritually blind and deaf. Its brief moments of pleasure obscure the fact that all who choose it and its ways choose a road filled with pain, torment, peril, and ultimately death, not only in this present world, but most especially, in the eternal one to come. On the other hand, those who embrace the Lord and His ways shall be rewarded in this present world with joy and inner peace (even while in the midst of extreme difficulties). Furthermore, in the world to come they will enjoy eternal life and never ending bliss in the presence of the Lord.

No Boasting/No Condemnation

However, none of us are worthy to boast or gloat, for we have all sinned against God. We have all been idolaters somewhat, for throughout our lives, we have placed ourselves, things, or other people before the Lord. That decision alone is enough to condemn us. It stands against us (as does all of our rebellion against the Lord) as evidence of our guilt before Him, testifying of the fact that we are all idolaters and anarchists who have willingly rebelled against the Kingdom of God and its King.

We have all stubbornly refused His right to rule us, choosing instead to live independently of Him. Therefore, we are all spiritual criminals. And, like those crucified with Jesus Christ, all of us are in need of Him and His mercy, grace, forgiveness, cleansing, restoration, and salvation.

If we refuse His right to rule and reign over us, we abide under a verdict of guilty and an unimaginably terrifying sentence of eternal death consisting of never ending torment, darkness, and gloom. In this horrible place, there is eternal separation from the God of light and life and His glorious kingdom of righteousness, peace, and joy.

But, even as we have no right to think ourselves less guilty or needy than others, neither should we succumb to the lie that says there is no hope for us. Even as one of the dying criminals who were crucified alongside our Lord Jesus Christ found salvation in Him, so can each one of us. My prayer is that you and I both will follow the example of the repentant ex-con, looking upon the Lord and our need for Him even as he did.

The Middle Man

Realize that the Lord Jesus Christ ("the Middle Man")—the only Mediator between God and humanity—was suspended between earth and Heaven as the only bridge between the two. With outstretched arms, He beckoned you, me, and everyone else to come to Him.

In His embrace, we will find the love and acceptance that we all long for so desperately. As the sacrificial lamb Who was provided by God Himself, He has paid the price for sin and fully met the demands of God's justice with His blood and death. He did this so thoroughly, even the record and memory of our sin stands ready to be removed, permanently washed away by His precious blood. It became the provision for our forgiveness, safety, security, and confidence before God. Now, His resurrection life is available to all who forsake their own lives that they might wholeheartedly seek Him and His desires.

Truly, the Lord Jesus Christ is our only hope and salvation.

We can partake of His life and enjoy everlasting friendship and fellowship with Him. But first, like the repentant criminal on the cross, we must humble ourselves. Opening our hearts, we must choose to receive Jesus Christ as Savior, surrender to Him as the Lord, and then obediently follow Him. We will find that if we will call on the Lord out of our need, He will answer us out of His sufficiency.

For if we will call out to God for mercy, it will be granted because Jesus Christ has taken our punishment for our part in The Rebellion.

Risen, Reigning, & Returning

Jesus' sacrifice of Himself totally satisfied the demands of pure, perfect, divine holiness and justice. Had it not done so, Jesus Christ would not have been raised again to life.

But, bless God, He is risen!

He is no longer on a cross or wrapped in the dark cloak of death. He has forever defeated every enemy of God and His pure, righteous ways. As the risen, reigning Lord and Savior, He ever lives to present us totally acceptable to God through His perfect and eternally sufficient sacrifice, made once for all.

How much we need Him!

If you haven't called out to Him, won't you do it now? Your time of anarchy can end today.

Right now.

The essence of sin is that we have all chosen to go our own way, to "do our own thing" instead of obediently follow God. Repent, that is, change your mind about the way you have lived independently of Him. Don't just be regretful for mistakes and wrong choices you have made due to a wicked heart. To admit these things is fine, but you must go one step further, back into God's waiting arms. In other words, you and I are called to turn *from* sin and *to* God.

Admit how you have gone your own way and that it was wrong for you to do so. Confess this to Him and tell Him that you give His Son the right to rule your life as your King. Let's not be as those in the preceding story who rejected the king's love and scorned his son. Instead, let us be like those who gladly accepted the king's right to rule them.

Don't put Him off a moment longer. While you still have the opportunity, open your heart to Him and acknowledge to Him how much you need Him. Accept the sacrifice of Jesus' life and sin-removing blood that have been poured out for you. Thank Him for dying for you and realize that He has been resurrected from the dead. The one and only Savior of humanity is risen and is alive forevermore. We don't have to settle for worshiping at the shrines of men's religious thoughts and efforts to honor a "dear" but dead religious teacher or idealist. The resurrected, ever-living King loves you and beckons to you to open your entire being to Him.

Give Him your all.

Love Him, and let Him love you.

Don't turn away from Him anymore.

Won't you now bend the knees of your heart (instead of only your body) before the King of creation?

If you will daily walk in obedience to Him, you will have nothing to fear on *The King's Day Of Reckoning,* for He has paid *The Price Of Freedom.*

God is calling people to Himself, but it shall not always be so. He has appointed a Day when He will judge everyone who has ever lived, either condoning or condemning them based on the lives they chose to live: Did they accept His Son and live lives that please Him by yielding to His Holy Spirit, following His leadings, and thereby "store up" and "invest in" "treasure in Heaven"? Or did they "blow their true, spiritual inheritance" and squander their lives away on what will amount to worthless, wasteful pursuits as far as eternity is concerned?

For those who will be found ready due to their acceptance of the sacrificial death of God's Son and by walking in His resurrection reality and power, there shall be eternal rewards: life and peace and an unfathomable, never-ending relationship with God.

But there will be a different, fearful fate for those who are self-seeking and will not turn from their selfishness to take up their crosses daily and follow Christ in obedient submission to His will. For them, there shall be the woeful consequences of incurring the wrath of Almighty God and suffering an eternity of the fate they chose while on earth—a damnation of self-absorption without hope. Why? Because, as they sowed in this life, so shall they reap in that which is to come—an existence without God.

Therefore, quickly now—we haven't much time left because soon the Judge will be calling—let us make certain that we are ready to stand before Him. We shall all stand before Him and our lives will be assessed, and *now* is the time to prepare.

Have we received Him and are we following Him, or not? Are we genuine disciples of Jesus Christ whose commitment to Him is evident by the lives we live? Or, are we just hypocritical actors who talk a fine line but do not walk the talk?

Remember our Lord's words: "Not everyone who says to Me, 'Lord, Lord,' will enter the kingdom of Heaven, but only the one who does the will of My Father Who is in Heaven.

"Many will say to Me on That Day, 'Lord, Lord, did we not prophesy in Your name, and in Your name cast out demons, and in Your name perform many miracles?'

"And then I will tell them plainly and publicly, 'I never knew you; depart from Me, you who practice lawlessness, disregarding My commands!'"

The Price Of Freedom has been paid against *The King's Day Of Reckoning.*

Therefore, while we have today, let us prepare for His coming…

for The Judgment…

for eternity…

for Him…

Following is a sober—even frightening—chapter that is not merely fiction with a message of no consequence. To the contrary, to ignore what it says to us would be folly and extremely costly, for this story contains much allegorical information concerning our relationship with the Lord. We would be wise to heed its warnings and lessons.

The Day of Judgment is approaching rapidly. Before God—the Holy One—each of us will stand and give an account for every thought, motive, word, and deed of our lives. Perhaps the following story will help us grasp this reality and the seriousness of our call to be loyal and faithful to Jesus, the King of kings and Lord of lords...

−10−

Lord, Lord!

Long ago, in a distant land, there was a wise king. Being a follower of the Lord Jesus Christ, he earnestly desired to rule his kingdom as the Lord does His. Therefore, he did so with justice and righteousness.

The time came when he took the pattern a step further: Knowing that the Lord will one day require everyone to stand before Him and give an account for the life they chose to live, this king ordered his subjects to be brought before him in order to be rewarded according to what they had done. As they stood before his judgment seat, he examined their love for him as well as their faithfulness and loyalty to him.

Eventually, a certain well-known and outspoken supporter of the king was summoned to the king's judgment seat. Almost everybody (including himself) thought that he would surely pass the intense scrutiny of the judgment with honors. Instead, his lack of being prepared was declared...

"But how can this be, O great king??? Why have I not been chosen to be a part of your inner circle? Why are you turning *me* away? These others that you've chosen over me...well...look at them! Most are not nearly as talented as I am. Few have labored so hard to bring you glory. Almost none of them knows your instructions and commands as well as I, nor does anyone study your edicts and insights so diligently. Who among them has told as many people as I have of your greatness, power, glory, and mercy? And if there is anyone who has (and I seriously doubt it), I'm certain they have not done so as eloquently or tirelessly as I. Why, O great King? Why, why, *why???"* the shaken servant sobbed through a deluge of tears.

The wise king looked steadfastly and tenderly at his subject, his deep, searching eyes filled with wisdom.

"The truth of much of what you say is undeniable," said the wise king. "And to many, you seem to stand head and shoulders above most of my other subjects."

The king leaned forward, looking intently at the distraught person before him.

"But you do not realize that I do not perceive the situation as most others. They are looking at mere externals—your outward appearance, but I am looking at your character, trying to discover fully what's in your heart with its unseen motives. Unfortunately, I have found selfish, hidden agendas in you. For you have lived for the applause and the praise that you could receive from others instead of me. You have loved the limelight for your own glory rather than serving me unselfishly with a pure, undivided heart."

The king paused for impact, letting his words sink in, then continued speaking his carefully chosen words with firmness, yet with kindness and compassion. "See these others that I have chosen and placed before you?" The king stretched out his right arm as he made a sweeping motion towards those to whom he was referring. He hesitated for a moment before continuing his explanation, and as he looked at his faithful, loyal ones with deep love and admiration, tears of joy and satisfaction filled his eyes.

Turning back to his trembling subject, he said, "Most of them, it is true, are not nearly as gifted as you, and few have worked so hard. But I am reminded of another one, many, many years ago, who stood taller than his peers—physically, that is. He was mighty before men and even before God when he walked in obedience to the Lord. God blessed him abundantly. He was honored and respected by many, walking in an authority given to him by God. However, his heart was not perfect toward the Lord, and he ended up choosing to do his own thing instead of continuing to serve the Lord with obedient love."

"And...and who was this...this...foolish one, O King?" the subject hesitatingly asked.

"His name was Saul, King of Israel," the king replied.

The quivering person gasped as he thought of the ill-fated King Saul.

"Remember, though he was so gifted and hard working, he met disaster because he turned from the Lord by refusing to obey His commands. In doing so, he rejected the Lord's authority and right to rule him. Saul stubbornly embraced his own ideas and the desires of other people instead of respecting and honoring God by walking in obedience to Him. In 1 Samuel 15, we read that the Lord then sent the prophet Samuel to Saul. In verses 22 and 23, we read these sobering words from Samuel to Saul, 'Does the Lord delight in sacrifices and outward show more than in obedience to his voice? Behold, to obey is better than sacrifice, and to heed [what God says] is better than to offer Him the [sacrifice of the] fat of rams. For rebellion is as the sin of witchcraft, and stubbornness is like iniquity and idolatry. Because you have rejected the word of the Lord, He also has rejected you from being king.'

"In spite of Saul's efforts and natural abilities, he and his sacrifices were rejected by the Lord because he chose to not love and honor the Lord by obeying Him. He was more interested in himself and *his* plans, prestige, and programs, than he was in bringing joy and satisfaction to God through his obedience to Him.

"Before the creation of man, even the once exalted angel Lucifer fell from his lofty place as an honored leader among the holy angels to become the leader of the rebellion against God and His authority. And what precipitated this tragedy? He got his eyes off his Creator, placing them on himself and on the glory the Lord had bestowed on him. Thus sin was born—the lie and The Rebellion began. Lucifer—the 'Light-Bringer'—

became known as Satan—the 'adversary'—and he was cast from his lofty position at the throne of God."

"Stop, O King, stop!" cried the servant. "Your words terrify me!"

"Rightfully so!" said the king, more firmly now. His eyes were flashing and his gaze seemed to penetrate the servant to his inner being. "Have I not said that my kingdom will be run as the Kingdom of God and that my subjects will honor me with selfless obedience, just as the Lord requires of me and all His other subjects? Well, your selfish pursuit of your own ways has placed you among the wicked ones like King Saul and Lucifer. Because of your self-centered rebellion, you will incur the same condemnation that came on them. For, like Saul and Lucifer, though you are gifted greatly, your heart is perverted. Your focus has not been fixed upon me and my purposes. You've become hardened against me, proud, stubborn, and you've squandered and wasted your gifts on your own self-glory."

"No, wait, O King!" interrupted the troubled servant. "I used my gifts for *you*. I used them to promote *your* kingdom!"

"Silence!" thundered the king. "That was often a problem with you. You have been quick to speak, yet slow to listen, and even slower to obey! Did you really think that merely mouthing my words was sufficient to please me? You may have known many of my words of instruction, yet you have despised them by not obeying them. That is like holding food in your hands yet refusing to eat it—it will give you no life and be of no benefit to you. And whoever despises my words, despises me, regardless of what they may 'claim.' "

The servant was speechless. Trembling almost convulsively, he fell in a heap before the angry king.

"Yes," the king continued, "you used your God-given gifts to tell others of me and *supposedly* to spread the influence of my kingdom to places both near and far, but it was not at my direction nor in my timing and was not really for *my* glory. Your self-sufficiency and independence did not benefit me or my kingdom. It merely served your own efforts to build up your ego and ultimately to promote your personal agendas and your own self-made 'kingdom.'

"Though many praised you and called you a loyal subject of mine, I account your so-called 'service' as nothing but acts of rebellious treason. You got what you were after—the approval and the applause of men—but you did so at the peril of forfeiting your opportunity to faithfully serve your king and ultimately rule with him.

"Promotion is in my hand. Had you been a loyal servant—living, as you swore to do, for my glory and purposes—I would have placed a crown upon your head and allowed you to reign with me on my throne, just as the King of Kings will reward His faithful ones. As it is, all you have are vain and quickly disappearing memories of men's accolades. You'll get none from me, for I know that your heart is not right before me. Your hypocrisy, deceit, selfishness, and self-glory are intolerable to me."

The king grew even firmer still.

"It is true that most of these others that you have insulted and looked down upon were not as talented or energetic as you, but they *loved* me. They earnestly desired and depended on me and looked to me for guidance as well as the means to accomplish my directives. Then they eagerly carried out only *my* will—not a polluted mixture of my desires mingled with their own.

"Only those who have proven themselves faithful to me by following my directions are worthy to be called loyal and mature. These are the called and chosen, proven to be developed enough to be placed in my household as mature sons, no longer to be treated as mere servants. Though they were unimportant in your estimation, they were made great by my power that I gladly bestowed on them because of their humility, their love for me, and the wisdom to admit that they needed my help. For the only ones who truly bring acceptable glory to me are those who look expectantly to me, using my resources to serve me. Those others like yourself who 'do their own thing'—who depend on their own power and ingenuity—do not please me or bring me glory. To the contrary, they incur my disappointment—even my wrath and disgust.

"Now that the day of reckoning has come, those whom you have despised shall walk with me and shall reign with me, for they are worthy and have overcome. They are worthy and overcame their enemies because they depended on *me,* looked to *me,* and obeyed *me.* They did not merely try to prove something to me by relying on their own strength and ingenuity. Because they depended so entirely upon me, I helped them to become what I desired them to become and to accomplish those things that I purposed for them to do. They laid down their own lives by turning from their own pursuits and agendas so that they could fully do my will. And now, as I promised them, the reward—of which they have often thought and for which they denied themselves lesser things that would distract them from their goal, the reward which seemed at times as though it would never come—shall be great indeed, even beyond their imagination."

Suddenly, the servant stopped his whimpering and crying. He jumped to his feet and, even with a hint of self-assurance, he blurted out to the king, "But, Lord, Lord, I also overcame. Besides telling others of Your Highness' great words of wisdom, I slew dragons in your name, O Great One! I *overcame* them, don't you see??? And I did other great and mighty works in your name, my Lord. For example, I..."

"O foolish one!!!" the king responded with finality.

The servant fell back, his face ashen, his eyes wide with shock and fear. Shaking uncontrollably and with sweat profusely pouring down his face, he haltingly asked, "Wh-Wh-What d-d-do y-you m-m-mean, O-O-O K-K-King?"

Kingdom Requirements

"You call me Lord, but your actions prove that you are a liar," said the king. Strong words are made empty, idle, fruitless, and useless by a weak life. I am Lord over those who willingly accept my lordship over their lives. As for those things of which you boast to have accomplished, you may or may not have done them. But you have not overcome that which is the real enemy to overcome (to the contrary, you have nurtured) that which would threaten both you, my other subjects, and my kingdom—

your own rebellious, selfish, independent self-love and self-will!"

The air grew still and heavy as these words echoed in the great Hall of the Throne of Judgment.

"You did not master sin that crouches at your door, even as Cain did not so many centuries ago. My true servants, like the servants of the Most High, must be teachable, and must esteem others as better than themselves. They must be willing and desirous to serve, seeking my pleasure before their own, even choosing to make my pleasure their pleasure. But selfish self-centeredness, self-promotion, greed, and lust motivated you. You did not love me—you loved yourself. You were not willing to put yourself aside so that my plans alone could be realized. When others looked at you, they did not see a well-disciplined and loving subject of the king who revealed my nature and character and who lived only to love and serve me—the one whom you *claim* to be your lord and king. No, on the contrary, they saw an opportunist who was full of himself and his own ways—the captain of his own fate. You were not willing to die to everything else but me, as my true and faithful subjects do. And now, 'captain,' your 'ship' is going down in flames, and you with it.

The man shrieked at these words.

The king continued: "O!—I would have taken care of you so much better than you could have ever taken care of yourself. But you did not trust me. You did not really love me. This has hurt and grieved me deeply, and your stubbornness and rebellion have stirred my anger. You see, you were too busy working *for* me, serving me (or so you say), but you never came to me and waited for my directions as I have so clearly instructed my subjects to do. I promised those who proved their devotion to me by obeying my personal directives to them that they would be welcome in my courts to confer with me and sit at my table. But you never experienced such intimacy with me because you never truly desired to know me. You were called to be with me, but you refused my call. Now, you will not be chosen by me because you did not choose me."

"But I was in your service, Your Majesty," the trembling man cried, "telling others about you and your proclamations! I...!"

The king held up his hand to incur silence, then continued, "Oh yes, you spoke *about* me and studied things that I have declared, but you never had a true relationship *with* me, though I longed for this and urged you to do so your whole life. I often sent for you so that you could spend time with me. I waited and waited, but you rarely came to me. You were too busy doing your own thing even to care to notice my calls, much less obey me. You were more interested in what you thought you could do in my name than in really coming to know the one behind the name. You sought your own glory and to make a name for yourself in a self-centered kingdom of your own making. You did not live for my glory and the honor of my name and kingdom. Settling for a minimal awareness of me and my ways, you never allowed me to be anything but a stranger to you in your daily life. Therefore, you stand before me now—a stranger.

"You never comprehended (nor did you ever want to comprehend) that everything you endured, every task I assigned to you, was designed as a test to develop a genuine and solid character in you that would display my own standards and to prepare you to share my throne with me.

"You know that I have patterned my kingdom after the Kingdom of kingdoms, and from His lofty throne, the King of kings has required that everyone, including me, must turn from their own pursuits and their self-absorption that causes them to live only to please themselves. Everyone must recognize that their righteousness—all their supposed 'goodness'—is as filthy rags before the Holy, Living God. Acknowledging that we are helpless apart from Jesus Christ and are desperately in need of His sin cleansing, forgiving blood, we must live in total dependency upon Him and for His purposes alone.

"He has shown us all that we must not settle for a form of godliness instead of having our hearts transformed by His Spirit. Having relationship *with* Him is key, not merely having religion *about* Him. We must not settle for rituals and forms—mere outward displays that at best only remind us of Him. Instead, we must know Jesus Christ—He Who is the power of godliness. Seeking Him, loving Him, and growing in a deep and intimate knowledge *of* Him (not just *about* Him) is the only way to overcome the hypocrisy of empty, put-on religious show. The ability to live righteously, enjoy Him, and bring joy to Him forever must flow from relationship with Him. Through our union with Him, He equips and energizes us to both desire and do His will.

"Similarly, I wanted you to come to me in recognition of your need of me and with an understanding of my kingdom that went deeper than head knowledge. I desired that you allow this truth to enter into your heart and transform your character. If you had, I would have gladly responded by helping you in every way that you needed. But, you were not willing. Instead of being dependent upon me, you relied on your own ingenuity, strengths, and natural talents.

"In short, you were self-sufficient. Unfortunately, your self-sufficiency is your insufficiency. It is your undoing.

"Now it is too late. Your rebellious independence is totally intolerable, belligerent anarchy. Knowing my will, you nevertheless chose to go your own way and do your own thing, and this is iniquity. Only those who are mine—not only in their minds and mouths, but also in the motives and deeds of their hearts—will remain with me. These are the ones who obey me, the ones I really know and call by their names. Your so-called 'relationship' with me was nothing more than a distant awareness you had of me.

"So now I pass this sentence of justice on you:

"I never knew you! Guards, remove this stranger from me and my kingdom. Cast this foolish one and his works into the fiery pit!"

"No! N o ! N OOO ! " the man screamed as he fell on his hands and knees, sobbing. "Besides, I'm...*I'm* not foolish!!!"

"On the contrary," said one of the king's mighty guards as he took the man away, "you are more than foolish. Your time is past, the judgment has come and gone, your guilt remains, and you are not ready. Now, it is forever too late and you will not be saved. For whoever is without the king is also without hope."

Just before the huge doors to the Great Hall closed, you could hear the man weeping and wailing, "Not me! Look at *me!* I've got it together...I'm your greatest and most faithful servant! Lord, LOOOOOOOOOOOORD!!!"

Mere lip service is not enough; loudly *professing* faith without *possessing* it will not do. Genuine, saving faith is more than just admitting that we believe some facts that we were told. Instead, it is a complete rolling over of all we are onto Jesus Christ and relying on Him totally to make us acceptable to God through His blood, death, and resurrection from the dead. Furthermore, it is visibly evidenced by a sincere pursuit of God and living in obedience to what He reveals.

Matthew 7:21 reveals that the eternal kingdom of the Lord Jesus does not await those who cry "Lord, Lord," while doing their own thing. As Luke 9:23 and 14:26-35 declares, all true disciples of Jesus Christ must deny themselves and obey what He says.

Many speak loudly of Jesus before men to be seen by them, yet they actually deny Him and bring reproach to His name because they are not led by His Spirit and therefore do not live according to His standards. Romans 8:13-14 tells us that "...if you live according the dictates of the flesh you shall surely die. But if through the power of the Holy Spirit you are habitually putting to death the misdeeds of the body, you shall live. For all who are led by the Spirit of God are sons of God." 1 John 2:4 tells us that whoever claims to know God but does not obey Him is a liar, and the Truth is not in him.

In Luke 6:46, Jesus said, "Why do you call Me 'Lord, Lord,' and do not do what I say?" The Revelation 20:11-15 and Romans 2:16 reveal that many will cry out for mercy on the great day of God's Judgment when He will judge everyone according to the things they have done and the secrets that they conceal. As a defense, they will bring up the times when they spoke to others on His behalf, the times when they had victory over satanic forces through His power, and the times they did other mighty deeds while claiming to be His representatives. Nevertheless, we need to heed the warning of Matthew 7:21-23. In this passage of Scripture, He reveals that He will harshly judge all hypocrites, casting them from

His presence because they would not relinquish their selfish pursuits for *His* interests, and they did not truly desire closeness with Him.

Read And Take Heed

Hear as He speaks to those who would follow Him: "I have loved you just as My Father has loved Me, but you must make a continual choice to abide in My love by obeying Me. Only those who follow My leading, obeying My voice, are My friends, and only those who choose to seek out and obey the leading of God's Holy Spirit and the instructions of My Word will know the joys and fulfillment of being known as God's children. [Romans 8:14.]

"Do not take lightly My mercy that I have extended to you. If it was not for My choosing you, you never would have come to Me, for in and of yourself you would have no inclination towards the Truth. [John 6:44.]

"I have not called you without a purpose. You are to be a living testimony before others concerning Me and My kingdom, not only with words, but with a consistent life of good deeds. [Ephesians 2:10.] You must see to it that by My Spirit you not only 'talk the walk,' but that you also 'walk the talk.' This will occur only as you have pure motives and humble, teachable hearts that sincerely love and seek Me, not attitudes full of gall and guile and proud self-sufficiency.

"You are like a branch that must stay attached to a vine in order to bring forth life. As I taught in John 15:1-8, 'I am the Vine; you are the branches.' You will undergo cleansing by God's Word, and it will sometimes be painful, seemingly cutting back what you have to offer. However, know that My Father, like a wise and caring gardener, is merely 'pruning' you, so to speak. He desires to make you better suited to bring forth even more life and more excellent fruit.

"Also, His pruning is infinitely more to be desired than His rejection due to resistance and lack of response to His dealings. Therefore, choose to respond positively to My Father's dealings, following Me in word and deed. The more you are in love with Me, the easier and the more joyful is your responsiveness and obedience to the Spirit of God.

"However, don't substitute works for relationship. So-called "good things" are not necessarily "God" things. Doing even supposedly good things in an attempt to testify in My behalf are not acceptable to Me if they are done apart from vital union with Me.

"Do not be deceived concerning this.

"Your works do not produce good standing with Me. Instead, they are to flow out of an established, ever-deepening relationship that we have. Remember: Works do not produce relationship with Me, but relationship with Me will produce works.

"These works that are pleasing to Me will occur as you respond to My Father's working within your hearts. As it is written in Philippians 2:13-14, '...continue to work out your own salvation with fear and trembling.' Yet, do not attempt to do this in your own strength, for '...it is God Who is at work in you—energizing and creating in you the power and desire—both to will and to do His good pleasure and satisfaction and delight.'

"Therefore, realize that a real union with Me will produce good works as a matter of course. It is your response to My Father's ability—His transforming grace—that enables you to do His will. You 'work out' what He has first placed within you. This understanding will help to keep you focused on the God of the labor rather than on laboring for God.

"Whether or not you are led by My Spirit to do things that others applaud is not the critical issue. It is not so much what you've done in My name, but rather: Are you available to Me to do with you as I will? Do you know Me intimately? Are you getting to know Me better?

"Knowing that your relationship with Me is a gift from God and not something that you can ever earn prevents you from being able to boast that you deserve God's notice or mercy. For all people deserve death, but God is merciful."

Hearers—Not Just Doers

Let us therefore examine ourselves, making certain that we are abiding in the faith just as 2 Corinthians 13:5 exhorts us to do. Our hearts are to be set continually on pleasing the Lord, pursuing His kingdom, always choosing the way of obedience, and coming to really know Him in an intimate, personal way.

If we notice a lack of concern on our part regarding seeking the Lord or desiring to please Him, we should not hide the true condition of our hearts. Instead, we need to acknowledge our sins and weaknesses to Him and to other trusted believers. [1 John 1:9; James 5:16.] It is foolish and dangerous for us not to face up to the truth and attempt to hide our hearts' true condition, whether through secrecy or by pretending to be something that we are not. God sees all things and will one day reveal all things by bringing everything into the light. If we attempt to deny or hinder the truth of what is within our hearts and minds (even if it be embarrassing to us), we further open ourselves to darkness—if we refuse light, we embrace darkness.

We also need to guard against the subtle deception of thinking we are all right just because we're involved in ministry, including prophesying, casting out demons, and doing many mighty works in the Lord's name. The Lord would rather have to deal with weaknesses and wickedness that are honestly faced and confessed, than pretentious, fake, so-called "spirituality." He would even rather deal with an honest sinner than with a dishonest saint.

If we are honest with the Lord and yielded to Him, He will work within our beings a desire and an ability to walk in genuine holiness and to accomplish His will at all times. For, as James 1:22-25 points out, we must be doers of God's word, will, and way, not hearers only, thereby deceiving ourselves.

Remember John 14:21. There we read of Jesus saying that whoever truly loves Him obeys Him. As Matthew 7:21 reveals, merely crying out *"Lord, Lord,"* to Him will only add to our condemnation if we do not *do* what He says.

Have you examined yourself to see if you are in the faith, just as we have been exhorted to do in 2 Corinthians 13:5? Are you truly a disciple of the Lord Jesus, or has the Holy Spirit revealed to you that you are a "counterfeit Christian"—one in name only whose heart is not right with God?

If you pass the scrutiny and searching eyes of the Holy Spirit, I rejoice with you. Yet, even if you realize that you are not truly one who belongs to the Lord, I encourage you not to despair. Allow me to introduce you to the King—the Lord Jesus Christ. Everyone needs Him...*desperately.*

He is the One Who so kindly forgave me for my great stubbornness and rebellion against Him and His ways. Believe me, if He is willing to forgive me, He is also willing to forgive you.

The acknowledgment of our needs is the first step to getting them met. Our acknowledgment of bondage is the first step to seeing it broken and its shackles removed. And our willingness to let go of the right to rule our lives is the first step to being able to lay hold of Jesus Christ as our Life.

He loves you so much that He willingly left the glories of His celestial kingdom in Heaven to lay down His life for you, taking the punishment each of us deserves. Having been raised from the dead, He is beckoning you to turn to Him. Allow Him to cleanse you from The Rebellion and its ways. He is ready to forgive you if you are ready to accept His gift of salvation and follow Him in loving obedience and devotion. For, although we cannot earn salvation, He requires that all people submit themselves fully to Him in order to receive Him and the freedom that He offers us from the penalty, power, and practice of sin. He is willing to lead us *if* we are willing to follow Him.

Hosea 14:2 says, "Take with you words, and return to the Lord." The following words may help you to express your needs and the longings in your heart to Him. Pray what is written or merely use them as a guide and pray to Him in your own words:

"O Lord God, I confess to you that I am a sinner because I have stubbornly chosen to go my own way and do my own thing. I have not submitted myself to You. I have done my own thing. I have turned from the way that is right—the way of light—and have plunged headlong into the ways of night. In so doing, I have both hurt and offended You and others. I have been wrong. I repent of these. Please forgive me, Lord.

"Thank You, O God, for loving me so very much that you even sent to earth Your Son, Jesus Christ, to offer Himself as the perfect and final sacrifice to pay the penalty required for my sin and all of my rebellious thoughts and prideful acts.

"I confess that Jesus Christ is Lord and the Son of the Living God, that He came to earth in a physical body, sacrificed His blood and body for my sin, and was raised from the dead by the power of God. I believe that because of His obedience to God and the sacrifice of His holy, sinless life, I can be forgiven for all my disobedience to God and for my unbelieving, unholy, sinful life. In its stead, I know that I am to live a life dedicated to God and full of the power that raised Jesus from the dead.

"I acknowledge that He is the only way to You, and I also confess that You, O God, raised Him from the dead, never to die again.

"I now turn from and renounce The Rebellion in all of its forms so that I can give myself completely to God and follow Jesus Christ as My Lord and Savior. I no longer want any part of The Rebellion.

"I fully repent and turn to You, O God and give You complete rule over my life. I renounce every opportunity I have given the enemy in my life and I drive him out of me and away from me, in Jesus' name. I shut every gateway of entrance for the devil and his angels in my life. I renounce Satan and all of his works such as all sexual uncleanness and perversion done to me and by me, all witchcraft including tarot cards, Ouija© board involvement, and all other forms of the occult. I forgive all who have done me wrong so that You, my Lord, will forgive me for all the wrong that I have done. I confess and renounce all involvement with uncontrolled wrath, rage, all bitterness, stealing, murder, evil, mean, or filthy talk…"

[At this time, continue to speak forth things that the Lord brings to mind, regardless of how repulsive to you and difficult to admit. For some, this will only take a few moments. For others, it will take quite a while. Either way, know that God will help you. He wants you to have a purified conscience and a pure, clean heart. As you follow through with all of this, holy and unholy angels alike will be made aware of your renouncement of Satan and his ways and of your acknowledgment that you have been purchased for God by the blood of Jesus Christ His Son.

You may want to write down a list of things, if you feel this would help you say all you would want to say. Don't be bothered if you can't remember much that you may possibly like to confess to God. He will bring it to your memory if you need to confess it. Just trust Him. He will lead and guide you. He has brought you this far, and He's not about to forsake you now. He loves you and accepts you because He accepts you in Jesus, His beloved. In Him you, too, are beloved. Let Him have His way in this time of confession. Then, continue…]

"Take me, Lord God. Cleanse me and change me. O God, I open up my whole being to You. Search me thoroughly and remove everything that would hinder You from having Your way in and through me. I give up the right to rule myself and all my rights to You. Please fill me with Your precious Holy Spirit, anointing me so that I have the power to do only Your will, and to do it fully.

"How I need You, Invisible God. There is no other God besides You. You are holy and great. Thank You for hearing me. Thank You for saving me from death and Hell and for filling me with Your Holy Spirit. I know that You have done this because I have asked as one who is now your child. Yes, You are my *Father—my Daddy!*"

"How I need You, Lord Jesus and love and thank You for obeying our Father by taking upon Yourself what I was due to suffer. I was the one who went astray, but You took the punishment for it. I deserved to die for my sin, but You took my place, dying for me. You gave Your life in exchange for my spiritual death, and I am so very grateful. Thank You for Your precious blood that cleanses me from all that displeases God.

"Praise Your great and mighty name! There is no one like You, precious Lord. Hallelujah! Thank You, Jesus!"

If you cried out to God and called on the name of Jesus in submission to Him as Your Lord, He heard and received you. He will never reject those who truly turn to Him. As He Himself said in John 6:37, "All whom My Father has given to Me will come to Me; and whoever comes to Me I will most certainly not cast out—I will never, no never reject one of them or drive away whoever comes to Me."

I rejoice with you if you have given your all to the Lord Jesus. May you continue to remain open to Him and obediently responsive to His Word and His Holy Spirit.

[Be open to contact all offended, wounded parties for different provocations as soon as possible and apologize to them. Repay, if possible, anything you have stolen in your previous state of rebellion.

Remember to bless those who curse you and do good to those who would treat you badly. Follow in the steps of the Master and fulfill the injunction of Romans 12:21—do not be overcome with evil, but overcome evil with good.]

Regardless of whether you have just now given yourself entirely to the Lord or have been walking with Him for many years, know that there is a fathomless "pool" of wisdom, of revelation, and of the knowledge of God that awaits your exploration. Every need is met; every holy desire is fulfilled in these pure waters.

The contents of these waters are beyond imagination.

Beyond our loftiest dreams.

Beyond what we can even comprehend are "the unsearchable riches" within this pool—this Person—Jesus Christ.

As we come to know Him, we shall know all we need to know and even do all that we should do. And one glorious day, we shall find ourselves in our Heavenly Father's arms and gazing into His eyes.

Come, let us forever plunge into the depths of God...

—11—

Wonder Of Wonders

Most of us have heard about "the wonders of the world." But there is something that is by far the deepest of all depths, the greatest of all knowledge, the most awesome and wonderful wonder of wonders in all of creation.

It is the unique, matchless calling from the Creator to everyone to know Him intimately and become united with Him—joined to Him by His Spirit. In fact, if the message of the Bible could be summed up in one word, I believe that word would be "relationship." God has always desired and sought relationship with a people who love Him for Himself and unreservedly love each other with purity. His heart is thrilled with those who seek His face more than they seek His hands. James 4:8 tells us that He draws close to those who draw close to Him. He likewise takes delight in those who love others as they love themselves—caring for them and looking out for their best interests.

Relationship with God is similar to relationships that we have with one another. Our relationship with Him is strengthened as we acknowledge Him, spend time with Him, and seek to develop a caring, friendly, honest rapport with Him. Jesus Christ our Lord has promised in John 14:21 and 23 that an intimate relationship with Himself and his Father will be granted to all who obey Him.

Knowing God is a knowledge of the heart that goes far deeper than mere "head knowledge." It goes way beyond regimented, empty forms and the externals of religious ceremony and ritual. What these can only at best symbolize, He offers us in the reality of genuine relationship with Himself that transforms our characters. As we experience His precious Presence, all of the vain traditions of men are shown to be lacking in substance and are swept away in His glory.

Another person cannot give the reality of experiencing God to us—we have to experience Him for ourselves. We can know *about* God from others, but to know *Him* really (not just things *about* Him) requires that we encounter Him and respond to Him individually.

This gift of gifts of real relationship with the Living God and His Son Jesus Christ is what eternal life really is. Rather than simply being thought of "a never-ending life," eternal life is best defined as "a never-ending relationship with the Living God and Jesus Christ His Son, through the workings of the Holy Spirit." As our Lord Jesus Himself has said in John 17:3, "And this is eternal life: to know (to perceive, recognize, become acquainted with and understand) You, the only true and real God, and to know Him, Jesus Christ, Whom You have sent."

Jesus—Our Pattern

Like everything else in our life in God, our ministry to others is to be an outgrowth of relationship with Him. As our hearts are set upon Him, then the life and love that we enjoy with Him will flow from us to others.

Our Lord Jesus, while truly and deeply caring people, was not motivated to minister to others primarily out of love for them, but out of love for God His Father. And because of His great, honoring love for His Father, He only did what He saw the Father do, He only said what He heard the Father say; in short: He always and only did what pleased His Father. His meat, His food, His sustenance was to do the will of His Father and complete the work that His Father had given Him to do. [See John 4:32; 5:19, 30; 7:28; 8:28-29; 12:49; Psalm 40:7-8; Hebrews 10:7.]

Even our Lord's sacrificial death for His fallen creation was based on His love and commitment to God, not to His creation. We see this in Luke 22:42, where we read that the day before His crucifixion, our Lord asked His Father to let Him not have to endure what was about to happen to Him, but He then declared that He wanted to do His Father's will, not His own. It was the Father's will that Jesus go through the indescribable difficulties and agonizing, tortuous traumas He encountered. Our Lord struggled with this, but willingly complied.

As we consider these things, we need to keep in mind that rather than weakening our love for our fellow man and duty before God, such a burning passion for God and pursuit of Him alone will only enhance and perfect all else because the greater includes the lesser. If we are truly committed to God, we will fulfill the wonderful, loving will of our Father far better than we ever could if our eyes and heart were simply set on doing good things.

Also, our submission to one another will be pure and unfettered with the weights of human effort, rules, and regulations, if we will just submit completely to the Lord. Then *He* will see to it that we are in right order and relationship with one another. As Galatians 2:6 has revealed, the positions men hold within the church do not matter. Rather, what matters is the position *the Lord* holds within our beings. We must keep first things first. All other things will fall into place *if* we love the Lord fully, singularly, and purely.

Our Constant Pursuit and Need

Through the challenges of the circumstances of everyday life, He is teaching us to trust Him and yield to Him, totally obedient in all things, and not to seek our own pursuits and pleasures. He desires for us to be always moving in His perfect will. If we do, then we will be constantly pursuing Him and His kingdom.

As we draw all of our resources from Him, we are continually cleansed by His blood from the contaminating influences and control of "sin," which is "the missing of God's best or rebelling against God in any form (which of course includes attempting to live independently of Him)." [See 1 John 1:7; 3:4.]

How desperately we need Jesus Christ! We must trust Him completely, resting in Him because, for those of us that love and follow Him, He has become our very Life. As He revealed in John 15:1-8, just as a branch cannot bear fruit apart from the vine, neither can we reveal God's character and become what He's called us to be apart from union with Jesus Christ. We must keep our hearts set continually upon Him, pursuing His will with all the discipline, tenacity, single-mindedness, devotion, and focus of a committed soldier, a champion runner, or a diligent farmer, just as we are instructed to do in 1 Corinthians 9:24-27 and 2 Timothy 2:4-7. As we continue to look to Him and develop intimate relationship with Him personally through His word and in fellowship with His people, we are changed to become just like Him—what we love, we behold, and what we behold, like that we become.

Therefore, let's heed Hebrews 3:1 which tells us to keep our eyes on Jesus. To do this, we must turn our gaze away from the allurements of the world. Otherwise, we will take on the characteristics of the world and incur its judgments. [1 John 2:15-17].

In Luke 17:32, our Lord told us to remember Lot's wife. Genesis 19:26 reveals the tragic result of her failure to turn from this world. Instead of pursuing God's will with a fixed and determined focus, she disobediently turned to look back longingly at that which God had cursed and condemned. Her body was no longer in a place of compromise, but her heart and mind certainly were. She had gotten out of the evil, but she was not willing to allow the evil to be removed from her. Because of her disobedience and idolatrous lust, she perished in the destruction of the evil that she loved and chose to cling to in her heart.

Yes, may we always remember Lot's wife, lest we love and cling to what is cursed and therefore be cursed ourselves, perishing with it.

Moses Saw God's Ways—Not Just His Acts

May our walk and relationship with God be as that of Moses instead of the other children of Israel. Psalm 103:7 says, "He made known His *ways* to Moses, His *acts* to the children of Israel." Exodus 33:11 reiterates, "The Lord would speak to Moses face to face, as a man speaks with his friend."

This precious fellowship with the Living God that Moses enjoyed was not just because of God's sovereign election. In Numbers 12:7, the Lord tells us that Moses was "...faithful in all My house." And because of that faithfulness, the Lord said in verse 8 regarding Moses, "With him I speak face to face, clearly and not in riddles; he sees the form of the Lord."

Moses witnessed the acts of the Lord, just as the rest of the children of Israel, but because he maintained an intimacy with the Lord due to his faithful obedience, Moses also was shown the Lord's *ways,* while the rest of God's people were not.

Do we desire the Lord to reveal His ways to us as He did with Moses instead of only His acts? Then we, like Moses, must prove ourselves to be faithful to do God's will.

Fellowship First, Then Works Will Follow

If we maintain close fellowship with the Lord, then works that are born of His Spirit will follow. Real relationship with God results in real righteousness—attitudes and deeds that are always born of God. We must remember that the focus is to be on the Lord Himself, not on all the things we may want to do for Him. Genuine relationship with the Lord will produce righteous works—not the other way around.

The Living God does desire that we see and participate in the demonstration of the Holy Spirit and of power. [1 Corinthians 2:4; 14:1.] However, He is far more pleased to see mature, righteous character developed in us than to see us do mighty deeds. He has called us to develop and maintain intimate fellowship with Him, walking in "the secret of the Lord," of which Psalm 25:14 speaks. Though His plan is to display His power through His people [Daniel 11:32; Mark 16:17-18], we need to stay aware of God's ultimate goal (mentioned in Romans 8:29) of inwardly transforming and conforming us into the image of His Son. In other words, God wants to see the nature of Jesus His beloved Son revealed in and through us. Furthermore, the cleaner and less contaminated the vessel, the more readily and clearer will the indwelling glory of God be revealed in and through it without mar or taint.

This godly character of Jesus Christ that is produced in us as we depend completely on Him is more valuable to God than natural strength. Inner, spiritual strength and beauty is far more greatly esteemed by him than outer, physical strength and beauty.

As He reveals in Proverbs 16:32, "He who is slow to anger is better than the mighty, and he who rules his spirit than he who takes a city." What we are will ultimately determine what we do, and there certainly is nothing wrong in accomplishing great things in union with the Spirit of God. However, the Lord would have us get our eyes off of His manifested power and "demonstration," and place them completely and totally on Him. His ideal is for His mighty acts to occur as a result of our fixed focus on Him, as "supernaturally natural offshoots" of our perception and pursuit of the highest Goal—God Himself.

Like Daniel 11:32 declares, "...the people who *know their God* shall be strong, and carry out great exploits." The focus is on knowing Him. Then, strength and exploits will follow; not the other way around.

If we genuinely desire to know the Lord intimately, we must be certain to seek God's face in total truthfulness, persistent purity, and obstinate obedience to Him. His Holy Spirit is eager to enable us to do these things. By His strength, we can pursue the Lord with diligence, consistency, holiness, and love. [See Psalm 91; Proverbs 8:13; and John 14:21, 23.]

Our First Priority

The Lord Jesus said in Matthew 6:33, "...seek first the Kingdom of God and His righteousness, and all these things shall be added to you." In The Revelation 1:9, we discover that God's kingdom is found *in* Jesus Christ. Therefore, as we seek Him, we are seeking God's kingdom. As Hebrews 12:2 says, He is "the author and finisher of our faith," and, as Jeremiah 23:5-6 reveals, as well as Jeremiah 33:16 and 1 Corinthians 1:30, Jesus Christ is also "Our Righteousness." As we remain focused on Him, all that we could ever need will be ours. Plus, we will be able to rest and rejoice in the most wonderful benefits of all in our life in God—intimate friendship, courtship, and union with God.

Who can comprehend it???—Jesus Christ has come to dwell in us through His Spirit. This is one of the main reasons (if not *the* main reason) that Jesus bears the title of "Immanuel"—meaning "God with us." Through His forgiving and equipping work accomplished through His death, His resurrection, and through the power of the Holy Spirit, Jesus has actually joined Himself to us. He has united Himself with us—spiritually literally.

How privileged we are to be able to enjoy intimacy with Him and to have a part in His revealing Himself to His creation. Thank God for His Spirit Who enables us to be obedient to Him and deeply in love with Him (which prompts us to be persistent in our pursuit of Him). How wonderful it is that in Christ Jesus we can enjoy the highest calling of all—to have intimacy with God and be used by Him for the revelation of Himself and His purposes to others; in short, "to know God and, then—through the power of His indwelling Holy Spirit—to reveal God."

All of these wonderful, precious privileges are ours due to the love and provision of God and are found only in our Lord Jesus Christ. He is our Completeness, our Righteousness, our Life, and all else that God offers us—Jesus is our All in all.

For God loved the world so very much, He gave His best—Jesus Christ, His Precious Son—He Who most certainly is the ultimate and most wonderful "*Wonder Of Wonders.*"

The Righteousness Of God

*T*here are a lot of fine, upstanding citizens in the world who, though they live impeccably clean and decent lives in the eyes of others, will nonetheless be condemned to Hell for their rebellion towards God. If this is shocking to us, then we need to see more clearly just what is true righteousness.

Although righteousness is a requirement of forever abiding in God's Presence, it does not consist of us merely doing what people consider to be "good" deeds or living lives that outwardly appear to be morally upright. For example, the Pharisees and majority of the other Jewish religious leaders who were living during Jesus' incarnation and ministry on earth lived lives that many thought (especially themselves) to be exemplary models of righteous living. But our Lord blasted them for being hypocrites who worked diligently to appear to be holy to other people when in reality they were filled with inner, spiritual filth that was clearly evident to God. In Matthew 23:25-26, we read these frightening and scathing words from the lips of Jesus—He Who is appointed by God to soon be the Judge of all—"Woe to you, teachers of the law and Pharisees, you hypocrites! You clean the outside of the cup and dish, but inside they are full of extortion—prey, spoil, plunder—and grasping, greedy self-indulgence and excess. You blind Pharisee! First clean the inside of the cup and dish, and then the outside also will be clean." So we see that a lifestyle that seems to be righteous before men can be an abhorrent, filthy abomination before God that is strongly rejected by Him.

Isaiah 64:6 reveals that, in God's sight, *all* of *our* righteousness is as filthy rags. Therefore, it is obvious that we are incapable of producing genuine, God-pleasing righteousness. 1 Corinthians 15:22 tells us that all that is in Adam dies, whereas, all that is in Christ is made alive. Therefore, all that flows from us as a result of what we received from Adam—our natural life—is ultimately doomed to fail in His sight. If we never turn from our own ways and allow the Holy Spirit to join us to Jesus Christ, then we have no righteousness that leads to life, regardless of how high our personal moral standards may be or how pure our lifestyle may appear to be to other people.

Genuine righteousness declares us "not guilty" because of what Jesus has accomplished. Also, it is made manifest in holiness and good deeds by those who are His as He reveals Himself in and through them. Simply stated, according to Colossians 2:3, genuine righteousness is Christ Himself.

In other words, He doesn't just give us righteousness; He is our righteousness. Only as we receive Jesus, love Him, and obey Him by depending on the power of His Holy Spirit will His holy nature and perfect righteousness be manifested in and through us. It is His life within His people that prompts and empowers them to do good and acceptable deeds before God. As we obey Him by depending on His help, His righteousness is revealed through us. So, we see that genuine righteousness is a merciful gift of God to His people that must be "unwrapped" in their daily lives.

Everything God calls us to be or become is found in the Person of His Son—the Lord Jesus Christ. Yes, everything to which the Father ultimately calls us and everything He desires to give us is found in Jesus. We see this in 1 Corinthians 1:30, which reveals that God has made Christ Jesus "...our Wisdom from God, our Righteousness, our Consecration, and our Redemption." Verse 31 concludes the thought with a quote from Jeremiah 9:24, saying, "So then, as it is written, 'Let him who boasts and proudly rejoices and glories, boast and proudly rejoice and glory in the Lord.' "

Colossians 2:10 tells us that we are complete in Jesus Christ. Therefore, our confidence before God comes only as a result of our accepting His gift of life and forgiveness in Him Who is our very life. [Colossians 3:4.]

White Garments And Filthy Rags

In The Revelation 19:8, we read that the fine linen that the saints are wearing is "the righteous acts of the saints." We must reiterate again, however, that these "righteous acts" are not so-called "good deeds" that we initiate on our own, for—as is the root, so is the fruit.

Jesus tells us in John 3:6, "Flesh give birth to flesh; and what is born of the Spirit is spirit." Also, we have learned from John 15:5 that anything that we attempt to do apart from Him is accounted by Him as "nothing." Although other people may commend us for works wrought by the flesh, we must remember the words of our Lord in Luke 16:15: "...what is exalted and highly thought of among men is detestable and abhorrent (an abomination) in the sight of God." Sounds like "filthy rags" to me.

The white garments spoken of in The Revelation represent deeds that originate in God and are brought into being through us as we obediently respond to His leadings and depend exclusively on His power. They are considered righteous because of their Source of origin. They are not considered righteous acts in and of themselves apart from God. The issue is not primarily *what* we do, but from *Whom* we receive direction and empowerment to accomplish His will. His will *for* us and *through* us must be the result of his first working *in* us. For this to occur, he looks for our cooperation.

Romans 13:14 instructs us to "put on the Lord Jesus Christ." We are to clothe ourselves with Him. *He* is the garment of white. He is the righteousness of the saints.

1 Peter 2:9 declares that we have been called to declare the praises and display the virtues of God Who has called us out of darkness into His marvelous light. For all who have received Him, His indwelling Presence must be the Source from Whom all activity, ministry, even life itself, must flow.

Because of this, He alone can display His virtues. That is, He is the power of godliness, He is our ability, He is our righteousness, our very life, and only He can fulfill the will of God. We become expressions of God's will only as we abide in union with the Lord Jesus through our God-enabled obedience to His Word and Spirit.

Sin Conquered And Removed, Not Just Covered

His sacrifice is not a cloak for sin. Rather, His divine, resurrection power equips us with the ability to consistently walk in true, genuine righteousness and holiness, thus revealing His very life and nature. We can now walk above the snares of the world, the flesh, and the devil. If we make excuses for our moral failures, we are deceived and make a mockery of Jesus Christ and His cross. As 1 John 3:7 reveals: "Little children, let no one deceive you. He

who does what is right is righteous, just as He is righteous. He
who does what is sinful (who practices evil doing) is of the devil,
because the devil has been sinning from the beginning. The reason
the Son of God appeared was to destroy the devil's work." Through
Jesus, we can have victory over sin—the devil's work.

Some believe that God's grace precludes our having to live holy
lives—that is, because of His grace, we do not need to concern
ourselves with holiness. Such thinking is errant and makes a
mockery of the sufferings and death of Christ as well as the
teachings of Scripture. Neither does it even begin to lay hold of
the power that raised Him from the dead. Those who teach such
things leave their hearers with the impression that "God doesn't
see our sin—He only sees Jesus. So, it doesn't matter what we do."
Baloney! In Hebrews 12:14, we read, "Make every effort to live in
peace with all men and to be holy; without holiness no one will
see the Lord."

Also, Titus 2:11-14 reveals to us that "...the grace of God that
brings deliverance from sin and its curses has appeared to all men,
teaching us to say 'No!' to all ungodliness and worldly passions
and to live self-controlled, upright and godly lives in this present
age, while we wait for the blessed hope—the glorious appearing
of our great God and Savior, Jesus Christ, Who gave Himself on
our behalf that He might redeem us (that is, purchase our freedom)
from all wickedness and purify *for Himself* a people that are His
very own, eager to do what is good." Therefore, to the degree that
we are walking in sin, to that degree we are not walking in grace
and righteousness. If our righteousness is not evident, then it is
not real.

On the other hand, we need to understand that, although the
power to walk in visible, perfect purity is ours in Christ, we do
live in bodies prone to sin and still have mindsets that take time to
renew that have been trained in many ways in opposition to God.
Though this is no excuse for sin, it does give an answer as to why
even sincere disciples of Jesus Christ face struggles with sin. Know
that, if we sin, we have cleansing through the ever-effectual blood
of Jesus the Messiah. As 1 John 1:9 tells us, "If we confess our sins,
He is faithful and just to forgive us our sins, and to cleanse us from
all unrighteousness."

What a glorious promise!

Rejoice therefore, saint, for not only have you been given the enablement to walk in victory over sin, you also have such a gracious, merciful, and loving Lord that he has made a way for you to find cleansing and to remain in His good favor even when you allow sin to have victory over you.

Such kindness works to enthrall our hearts and endear Him to us, drawing us away from sin and into the arms of His precious, holy Presence.

Right Reasons Regarding Righteousness Reap Rewards

We have spoken of a real, visible righteousness that is first born in us by the Holy Spirit and the finished, perfect work of Messiah. It is then "worked out," as it were, through our willingness to follow the Lord Jesus and lean on Him for His ability to live in a manner pleasing to Him. However, in living lives of evident righteousness, we must see to it that what we doing is not for men's approval and applause. After all, what we are in secret reveals what we really are in our hearts. Our Lord gave us instruction in these matters in Matthew 6:1-18. In verse one, He says, "Be careful not to do your 'acts of righteousness' before men in order to be seen by them. If you do, you will have no reward from your Father in Heaven." Though this is true, it is not all He said about doing "acts of righteousness."

In fact, He encouraged visible, outward evidences of invisible, inner righteousness. For example, in Matthew 5:16, he tells us, "Let your light so shine before men that they may *see your good works* and glorify your Father in Heaven.

When we consider both of these passages, the message becomes clear: God is to be glorified through our holy lifestyles and good deeds that are evident to other people. We must, however, guard our hearts so that we do not do things in front of others to try to convince them that we are spiritual and holy. Our motives should always be to bring satisfaction and glory to God by being quick to obey Him in all things. So-called "righteous actions" that are done to be seen by men are bad and make God sad. But actions that are born out of our union with Him and obedience to Him (though maybe seen by men) are truly righteous, and they make Him very glad.

This is why it was stated earlier that if our righteousness is not evident, then it is not real. It's kind of like faith being dead without works (we read about this in James 2:14-26). As faith without works is dead, so is righteousness without works.

The Fruit of Righteousness

Our union with God is made evident by the fruit of righteousness that others partake of in our lives. Again, if a fruit tree is dead, it will not bear fruit, but, if it is alive, it will bear fruit. Also, the fruit of the Spirit is not merely some "right standing" we have in God regardless of our lifestyles. After all, holy hearts produce holy lives.

Remember 1 John 2:29-3:9, where we read such things as "...everyone who practices righteousness is born of [Jesus]"; "...in Him is no sin"; "No one who lives in Him keeps on sinning. No one who continues to sin has either seen Him or known Him"; "He who practices righteousness is righteous, just as He is righteous"; and "He who sins (who practices evil doing) is of the devil, because the devil has been sinning from the beginning. The reason the Son of God appeared was to destroy the devil's work *(sin)."* So, we see that if there is no visible, literal fruit of righteousness, then there is no genuine righteousness.

As a matter of fact, the "fruit" of the Holy Spirit, listed in Galatians 5:22-23, are all inner qualities of character that will be evident if they are really a part of us. We've listed them before, but it would be good to list them again. They are: love, joy, peace, patience, kindness, goodness, faithfulness, gentleness, and self-control.

Remember, in John 15:5, our Lord reveals that He is the Vine and we are the branches. If the tree is holy, even so will its fruit be holy. If we will abide in the Vine through our dependency on Him to save us and enable us to obey Him, then His righteous life will be flowing through us. In turn, this will cause us to bear the holy fruit of the Spirit—the sweet, edible, appealing fruit of righteousness.

Ephesians 2:10 informs us that "...we are God's workmanship, created in Christ Jesus *for good works,* which God prepared beforehand that *we should walk in them."* In other words, good works are important. So much so, they are a measurement of fruitfulness in Titus 3:14, where we read, "Let our people also learn to maintain good works, to meet urgent needs, that they might not be unfruitful." As we have previously stated, so-called "good works" that originate from us are unacceptable to God. However, it is also unacceptable if we are not responding to His leading to do those good works that He planned long ago for us to do in union with Him.

How glorious are the words of Romans 8:3-4: "For God has done what the Law could not do, its power being weakened by the flesh. Sending His own Son in the likeness or guise of sinful flesh and as an offering for sin, God condemned sin in the flesh (He subdued sin, overcame it and deprived it of its power) over all who accept that sacrifice, so that the righteous and just requirements of the Law might be fully met in us who live and move not in the ways of the flesh but in the ways of the Spirit."

Hallelujah! God has come to us in the Person of His Son, conquering sin and its curse for us in Christ's body on the cross of Calvary. [Galatians 3:13; Romans 8:1-4; 1 Peter 2:24.] The Holy Spirit joins Himself with those who submit to the resurrected Jesus as Lord, enabling them to live in true and genuine righteousness that is evidenced moment to moment in their daily lives. It is true and genuine because it is the actual righteous life of the Son of God Himself, produced in us through the power of His indwelling Spirit. [2 Corinthians 5:21; 1 Peter 2:9; 1 John 3:7.]

Jesus Christ is our Life, our Goal, and our Righteousness [See Colossians 3:4; Genesis 15:1; Ephesians 1:9-10; Philippians 3:13-14; and 1 Corinthians 1:30]. Therefore, if we are not walking in righteousness, we are denying Christ. We might have what 2 Timothy 3:5 refers to as "a form of godliness," yet all the while be denying Jesus Christ—the power of godliness. For, as we have seen, it is only by our receiving and depending on the powerful, resurrected Christ that we are enabled to walk righteously before God. He enables us to fulfill the requirement of the Law to love the Lord our God with *all* of our heart, soul, mind, and strength, as well as to love our neighbor as ourselves.

We are all weak in and of ourselves and in need of His cleansing blood. However, we should not embrace a fairly common doctrinal deception that tells us that we are going to sin the rest of our lives. Remember that our Lord came to destroy the devil's work. So let's not deceive ourselves. We are needy, but He is more than able and willing to equip us to do His will through His empowering grace.

Do not be deceived: If our lives do not reveal God's righteousness, then we are not righteous; our hearts are still wicked. If Jesus Christ is not evident *through* us, we need to seriously question whether or not He is even *in* us. He came to establish His holy kingdom in the hearts of His people. Are we displaying His virtues, or our vices? Are we full of ourselves, or are we full of His Holy Spirit?

On the other hand, we need to not allow ourselves or anyone else to put us on some sort of law or "guilt trip" in the hopes that by really "buckling down" and applying all of our energies and resources to our moral dilemma, then we surely will overcome Satan, self, and sin, and will then and only then really please our Father Who is in Heaven. This is simply not true, for there is nothing in us apart from the Lord that can satisfy the holy requirement of the Lord. We must have Him and the provisions He offers us in His Holy Spirit.

The law of love will work in us as we come to see how much God really loves us and what He has provided for us in Christ Jesus. *That* law at work in us will enable us to overcome the evil that would overcome us but from the merciful help and grace of God. We conquer only as we cease from trying to conquer that which our Lord has already defeated and stripped of power and then yield aggressively to Him, admitting not only our needs, but also His wonderful equipping so that we can do His will.

As the Spirit of God says in 1 Thessalonians 5:23-24. "...may the God of peace Himself sanctify you through and through; and may your spirit and soul and body be preserved sound and complete and blameless at the coming of our Lord Jesus the Messiah. Faithful is He Who is calling you to Himself, and utterly trustworthy, and *He* will also do it [fulfill His call by allowing and keeping you.] *Notice—He* will do it." Thank God, He enables us to work out and walk in that which He has already accomplished on our behalf. Therefore, we need to remember that the penalty for our pursuit of sin was fully paid by Christ so that the power to persist in righteousness might be fully met in us who cling to Him for His enablement to do so. As the Spirit of the Lord reveals in 2 Corinthians 5:21, "For our sake God made Christ to be sin Who knew no sin, so that in and through Him we might become endued with, viewed as being in, and examples of *The Righteousness Of God.*"

-13-

The Good News Is Bad News To The Flesh

I used to drive by what seemed to be a barren field. It looked tilled and furrowed but totally desolate. There was a particular night that I remember noticing it being as barren and lifeless as usual. However, the very next morning, as I passed the field, I could see a blanket of new, green shoots all over it. That which had appeared to be barren, dead, and desolate had actually been going through a preparation and metamorphosis to burst forth with new life. The seeds that had been sown in the field had not been sown in vain. Hidden beneath the surface, buried in the dark soil, the miracle and wonder of life had taken root, grown, and was born, as it were, out of death. Though the life within the soil was unobservable as it developed, it was nonetheless present and, eventually, could not remain confined and buried.

The field, instead of being a *tomb* of barrenness and death, was actually a *womb* of fertility and life—resurrection life—so to speak.

Although for awhile it seemed as though no seeds had even been planted, much less taken root, they played an integral role in the bringing forth of new life through their own death. As Jesus said in John 12:24, "...unless a kernel of wheat falls to the ground and dies, it remains only a single seed. But if it dies, it produces many seeds..."

As it is with the field, so it is with those who are faithful to the Lord. Though we may appear to be dead and barren, the Lord is doing a great, secret work within us that shall soon be manifested. Hallelujah!

The Revelation 2:10 reveals that those who are "faithful unto death" will be given the crown of life. This dying means more than just physical death. Though it may involve this, we also must "die" to our own agendas and plans in order to walk in obedience to the Lord Jesus Christ and fulfill His purposes. Our dying to self and to everything else that does not pertain to the kingdom of life and godliness will be the "soil" in which the "fruit" of the resurrection life of the Son of God will be developed and seen.

The Cost Of Discipleship

Many rejoice at the thought of salvation, as indeed they should. It is a blessing beyond description that we can experience salvation and be forgiven, transformed, empowered by God, and experience real and deep relationship with Him forever. Yet, in our zeal to receive for ourselves and proclaim to others the benefits and blessings that are in Jesus Christ, we must be certain not to overlook the absolute *necessity* of accepting and proclaiming His demands. We must recognize not only His promises and blessings, but also His *conditions* for receiving them.

But, as we consider His conditions of requiring our all in order to receive Him as our all, we must know that it is worth it. We need to see with eyes of faith beyond the present difficulties to the eternal reward of righteous, obedient faithfulness to the Lord.

As Paul wrote in Romans 8:18, "I consider that the sufferings of this present time (this present life) are not worth being compared with the glory that is about to be revealed to us and in us and for us, and conferred on us!" And, in 2 Corinthians 4:17-18, he reveals, "...our light, momentary affliction (this slight distress of the passing hour) is ever more and more abundantly preparing and producing and achieving for us an everlasting weight of glory—beyond all measure, excessively surpassing all comparisons and all calculations, a vast and transcendent glory and blessedness never to cease! Since we consider and look not to the things that are seen but to the things that are unseen; for the things that are visible are temporal (brief and fleeting), but the things that are invisible are deathless and everlasting."

With these glorious truths in mind, let us consider the requirements of the kingdom—the cost of discipleship:

In Luke 9:23, the Lord Jesus said, "If any person wills to come after Me, let him deny himself—that is, disown himself, forget, lose

sight of himself and his own interests, refuse and give up himself—
and take up his cross daily and follow Me." And in Luke 14:26 and
33, He said, "If anyone comes to Me and does not hate his [own]
father and mother [that is, in the sense of indifference to or relative
disregard for them in comparison with his attitude toward God]
and likewise his wife and children and brothers and sisters, [yes]
and even his own life also, he cannot be My disciple...So then,
whoever of you does not forsake—renounce, surrender claim to,
give up, say goodbye to—all that he has cannot be My disciple." He
also said in John 12:25-26, "Any one who loves his life loses it. But
any one who hates his life in this world will keep it to life eternal.—
Whoever has no love for, no concern for, no regard for his life
here on the earth, but despises it, preserves his life forever and
ever. If any one would serve Me, he must continue to follow Me—
to cleave steadfastly to Me, conform completely to My example,
in living and if need be in dying—and wherever I am, there will My
servant be also. My Father will honor the one who serves Me."

In Romans 8:13, the apostle Paul wrote to Jesus' followers, saying,
"So then, brethren, we are debtors, but not to the flesh to live [a
life ruled by the standards set up by the dictates] of the flesh. For
if you live according to [the dictates of] the flesh you will surely
die. But if through the power of the [Holy] Spirit you are habitually
putting to death—making extinct, deadening—the [evil] deeds
prompted by the body, you shall [really and genuinely] live forever."

In Matthew 10:37-39, we read these words from the Lord Jesus,
"Anyone who loves father or mother more than Me is not worthy
of Me; anyone who loves son or daughter more than Me is not
worthy of Me; and anyone who does not take up his cross and
follow Me is not worthy of Me. Whoever finds his life will lose it;
and whoever loses his life for My sake will find it."

And in Luke 14:25-33, He reveals that in comparison to our love
for Him, our love for others, including our own lives, should be as
hate. In verse 33, He actually says, "...any of you who does not
give up *everything* he has cannot be My disciple."

Speaking of our calling, in 2 Corinthians 4:8-12, Paul wrote, "We
are hard pressed on every side, but not crushed; perplexed, but
not in despair; persecuted, but not abandoned; struck down, but
not destroyed. We always carry around in our body the death of

Jesus, so that the life of Jesus may also be revealed in our body. For we who are alive are always being given over to death for Jesus' sake, so that His life may be revealed in our mortal body. So then, death is at work in us, but life is at work in you." He also said in 1 Corinthians 15:31, "I die daily [I face death every day and die to self.]"

And, lest some think that the preceding words from the letters to the Corinthians applies only to apostles, read 1 Peter 2:20-21, "But how is it to your credit if you receive a beating for doing wrong and endure it? But if you suffer for doing good and you endure it, this is commendable before God. *To this you were called,* because *Christ suffered for you, leaving you an example, that you should follow in His steps.*" He goes on to write in 3:9, "Do not repay evil with evil or insult with insult, but with blessing, because to this you were called so that you may inherit a blessing." And in 4:19, Peter says, "...those who suffer according to God's will should commit themselves to their faithful Creator and continue to do good."

Whew!!! Tough stuff—in fact, impossible stuff—for the flesh. But by our God's grace, we can more than merely endure such things; we can be more than conquerors! As Paul triumphantly declared in Romans 8:28, and in 35-38, "...we know that in all things God works for the good of those who love Him, who have been called according to His purpose...

"Who shall separate us from the love of Christ: Shall trouble or hardship or persecution or famine or nakedness or danger or sword? As it is written: 'For Your sake we face death all day long; we are considered as sheep to be slaughtered.' No, in all these things we are more than conquerors through Him Who loved us. For I am convinced that neither death nor life, neither angels nor demons, neither the present not the future, nor any powers, neither height nor depth, nor anything else in all creation, will be able to separate us from the love of God that is in Christ Jesus our Lord."

From these and numerous other Scriptures, we can see that God is serious when it comes to His high and holy expectations of those who are His. Indeed, the *Good News* is *bad news* to "the flesh" because the "life sentence" provided through the eternal salvation that is offered in the Gospel of Jesus Christ is also the "death sentence" to rebellious, selfish, independent-of-God self-centeredness. Our 'natural' reasonings and desires apart from a relationship with God and submission to Him do not find the "Good News" appealing or good at all.

We must have faith in order to "see" beyond this present life and its temporary, carnal gratifications. Then, joyfully we will be able to renounce the appeal and allurement of living in the flesh so that we can persistently live in the Spirit.

The Way To Life In God Is Through Death To Self

- Denying selfishness (the emptying of self)
  leads to fullness in God.
- To walk in the way of light,
  we must turn from the ways of night.
- To walk with God, we have to choose to not walk in step with
  the world, the flesh, and the devil.
  (You can't dance with the devil and keep in step with God!)
- If we desire to be spiritual, we must refuse to be carnal.
- Only as we turn *from* sin can we turn *to* Him.
- The principle of experientially knowing God's life:
  Death precedes resurrection.
- Only as we die to our own life can we be reborn to share
  in Jesus Christ's resurrection life.
- Unless we are willing to die to self, we will never live to God.
- Only by denying the flesh its selfish ways can we experience
  the fullness of the Spirit of God's loving, holy ways.
- If we refuse to *bear* a cross *now*,
  we will not *wear* a crown *then*.
- Satan wants to *take* our lives as we pursue selfishness,
  living for ourselves—supposedly—for we would actually be
  living for him.
- The Holy Spirit wants us to willingly lay down our lives,
  offering ourselves as living sacrifices [Romans 12:1] and
  live unselfishly for God's glory in a pure and persistent
  pursuit of Jesus.
- Satan intends to lead us *to* eternal death, but Jesus wants to
  lead us *through* death to eternal life.

Paul referred to the conflict between the ways of God and the flesh in Galatians 5:16-17: "...walk in the (Holy) Spirit—responsive to and controlled and guided by the Spirit, then you will certainly not gratify the desires of the flesh. For the flesh sets its desire against the Spirit, and the Spirit against the flesh; for these are in opposition to one another, so that you may not do the things that you please."

Thank God, however, that victory has been secured over all desires that oppose God's will. In verses 24 and 25, Paul speaks of this already accomplished victory over the flesh through Jesus Christ: "Those who belong to Christ Jesus *have crucified* the flesh with its passions and desires. If we live in the Spirit, let us also walk in the Spirit." Notice the words—"have crucified." They are past tense. This is not something that is yet to happen in the future. It has already taken place on Christ's cross. Through our spiritual identification with Him on the cross, in the resurrection, and in His ascension back to Heaven to sit at the Father's right hand, we partake of and participate in His victory over all the enemies of God and redeemed humanity. God sees those who accept His Son as being "in Christ," thereby sharing in His total and eternal triumph.

As we have seen, the very essence of sin is living independently of God. Another way to say it is: Sin is the existence of another's will in opposition to God's will. God will not tolerate His creation living independently of Him and His purposes. He has this right, you know. Besides, God is so loving and giving, His requiring our complete acceptance of His will is always for our highest good.

ALL For Him

However, although the Lord delights in blessing us and so often lavishes blessings and gifts upon us beyond our needs, His ultimate purpose for us is that we would be a people who gladly and willingly exist only for Him.

Creation does not center around us. Life is not about us. It's all about Him. As the old adage goes: "History is *His Story.*" He does not exist for our pleasure. Rather, The Revelation 4:11 reveals that we and all of creation were created for *His* pleasure—all is for Him.

As it says in Titus 2:14, "...Jesus Christ...gave Himself on our behalf that He might redeem us (that is, purchase our freedom) from all wickedness and purify *for Himself* a people that are His very own, eager to do what is good."

1 Peter 2:9, written to believers in Jesus, says, "...you are a chosen people, a royal priesthood, a holy, dedicated nation, a people *belonging to God* (His own purchased, special people)..."

We see that God's call of life to us is also the death sentence of fleshly tendencies to be driven by selfish, self-glorifying demands upon ourselves and others. Knowing this should not discourage us, because the end of our ways marks the beginning of His. Full surrender to Jesus Christ leads us through the experiencing of His salvation that is "to the uttermost," spoken of in Hebrews 7:25.

This is glorious for our inner man, but our flesh recoils at the thought of subservience to any other but itself. As our lord says in Matthew 26:41, "The spirit indeed is willing, but the flesh is weak."

*The Good News **Is** Bad News To The Flesh.*

14

The Requirement For Victory

(Larry T's Testimony)

*T*he Lord is certainly not limited to speaking to us only during designated prayer times or at certain locations. I remember one of the first times I recognized His voice—I was in the shower.

I was so thrilled at hearing such a distinct message from the Lord that I yelled to my roommate to come into the bathroom so I could tell him through the shower curtain what had just happened. It had been like a ticker-tape going across my mind. His words had come with such unexpected suddenness and clarity that I was startled. I remember pausing to try to understand what was happening and to let the words He had spoken to me sink in. This is what He had so clearly communicated:

"You can't experience a victory unless you go through a battle."

Wow! It had a tremendous impact on me, yet I didn't begin to comprehend those words fully until months later. The greatest and most intimate revelation of God I was yet to know was soon to come, but not until *after* God brought me through the most difficult time of my life I had ever experienced.

I was about to become a living example of the reality of those potent words: "You can't experience a victory unless you go through a battle."

From Knowledge About God to Knowledge Of God

When I was a child of three to five years of age, I was sitting in a Baptist gathering, and I was drawing or doodling during a sermon. Towards the end of the meeting, during an invitation to "come to Jesus and accept Him as Lord and Savior," I suddenly and unexpectedly felt at least two strong "promptings" or "urgings" that literally pulled on me to the point that I actually leaned forward twice in my seat. This immediately got my attention, for I was very aware that I wasn't doing this on my own. I turned to my mother and said, "Mama, Something wants me to go down front." She told me to go on, so I did. Moments later, the pastor led me in a prayer of salvation to receive Jesus.

For years after that, however, although I believed in God, my experiencing Him was what probably could rightly be called "nominal." Rather than having a burning heart that was consumed with really knowing or pursuing the Lord, I had more of a "cultural, Bible-Belt, go-to-church-and-smile" understanding. This tended more towards being "churchy" yet remaining unchanged inwardly; informed but not really transformed; and becoming skilled at maintaining a front rather than seeking God to confront me and deal with the issues in my life. At best, this approach to life nurtured a spiritually lax attitude. Therefore, the older I got, the more I drifted away from consciously and consistently seeking God in a serious, sincere way.

This began to change, however, when I was about fifteen or sixteen years of age. I suppose some would say I was a one of the "Jesus People"—those multitudes (typically youth) who comprised the "Jesus Movement." At that time (the early 1970's), I really began to seek the Lord earnestly. I also expressed a desire to Him to use me to wage war against the enemy. Much of my time was taken up with prayer groups and Christian meetings. My friends were all Christians and my life was centered around seeking Jesus. Things were going along pretty well. I even did quite a bit of ministry—witnessing, teaching, and using my musical talents in outreach and in worship.

Still, my hunger for more reality and intimate relationship with the Lord grew. Even while attending a Bible college for a brief time, I told God that He was like a distant uncle who was nice and gave me things, but not someone I really knew. He wasn't as real to me as I wanted Him to be. So, I began to ask Him to let me really know Him. I personally wanted to know the God Who revealed Himself in the Bible—the God of Abraham, Isaac, Paul, the Lord Jesus, and others in the

Scriptures who knew Him. I was desirous of genuine experience, not just heartfelt conviction.

The "Word Of God," But Not The God Of The Word

Oh, I was full of head knowledge about the Lord. I could quote much Scripture by memory. Many said that they had been blessed through my ministry. Nevertheless, though I was so full of knowledge about God and other things and so occupied with ministry outreaches, He showed me how void I was of Him. This was when I first began to realize that someone can be full of knowledge of "the Word of God" without knowing the God of the Word.

The time came when I felt a real need to get away alone for awhile and seek the Lord with prayer and fasting. While praying one day, I heard a voice in my mind say, "You're damned." I was totally shaken. I know that many would argue that it was the devil, not the Lord, who told me I was damned. Whether it was the Lord or Satan who spoke to me, of this I am certain: The Lord had His hand on me and used what I heard and the trauma that followed to bring me into a genuine relationship with Him. He is not looking for a people who are simply full of empty, religious rhetoric.

Almost simultaneously to hearing that voice, I began to see, at least in part, the real condition of my heart. A slow, relentless, painful, devastating, and even terrifying process turned mere "head knowledge" of the holiness of the Lord and my fallen, helpless condition apart from Him into "heart knowledge." In the days, weeks, and months that followed, it seemed as though all that had been taught *to* me about the Lord and my relationship to Him was being revealed *in* me. Mere theory and empty rhetoric was totally shaken. It was a personal taste of the final "shaking" spoken of in Hebrews 12:26-27 that shall one day overtake everything that is created and temporary, "in order that those things which cannot be shaken may remain and continue." Facts that had been placed in my head became Truth that was born in my heart. For example, instead of sin being a doctrine that I had merely learned and had even parroted to others, I saw the reality of sin *in me*. It shattered my self-confidence and left me broken, weak, and aware of my great, desperate, utter need of the Lord.

For about six months I could not find relief from an all-encompassing feeling of distress, terror, gloom, and doom that settled over me and grew more and more intense as time went by. There was an indescribable, heavy oppression by day and terrifying, tormenting nightmares by night.

Terrible Fear, Hopelessness, And Helplessness

I probably would be unable to convey fully the trauma and absolute terror that engulfed me as I realized I was helpless in myself to escape what I was convinced was the just condemnation of God. I clearly saw, not just heard, that I was a sinner who deserved the full extent of God's wrath and punishment for rebellion against Him. It was as though I had stood before the throne of God and had been justly condemned to an eternal, excruciating Hell. I literally wept, wailed, and gnashed my teeth in torment. Often, I screamed out to God, begging Him to have mercy on my soul. [It's amazing that neighbors didn't call authorities.] Sometimes, I even banged my head against the floor or wall in total hopelessness, despair, and anguish. I considered killing myself, but the thought came to me that the devil wouldn't let me die—he would just fill me full of demons to do his bidding...

Weird? Yes, but these were some of the things I faced at that time.

In Romans 7:18, Paul wrote that he knew that nothing good dwelled in his flesh. As I began to really perceive some of the loathsomeness of my own heart, I came to believe that I could have written that verse with just as much conviction as Paul.

All my knowledge, pat answers, and neat little clichés were shown to be futile when not energized by the Spirit of God. I saw that I did not deserve God's mercy and help, but oh!—I was so very helpless and in need of Him. I came to understand that apart from His mercy and grace, I did not have the ability nor even the desire to pursue Him as my salvation.

Other People Could Not Help

For awhile, I sincerely and intensely searched for help and consolation from other people. However, my efforts proved futile and of no avail. In fact, many times when others would try to help me, even by quoting Scriptures, it seemed as though they were skimming a rock on the surface of the ocean while I was sitting on the ocean floor—far from being affected. But I do thank God that there were those whom He raised up to keep in touch with me, intercede, and engage in spiritual warfare on my behalf against the onslaughts of the enemy. Afterwards, the saint who was most often used in this way to save my life became my wife. *[Thank you, Alice—my sister, my bride!].*

All doubt as to the reality of Jesus Christ's own claims to be the source of life, deliverance, and transformation for me and the rest of humanity completely disappeared. This occurred as the revelation took root within me that He alone was sufficient and able to save me. I saw that He is humanity's only hope and source of salvation from the wrath and judgments of God against sin. So, I began an earnest and intense seeking after Him, crying out to Him for mercy.

During this time, I came to the place where I felt certain that there was no hope. How *awful and terrifying* that feeling was! It was truly a taste of the torments of Hell.

Although I had lost all sense of hope, I knew that my only Hope was the Living God. Without His intervening mercy and grace, I was doomed—eternally. So, I continued crying out to Him. I became very much aware that there was no higher appeal to Whom I could beg and plead for mercy. No one else could save me. I clearly saw that Jesus Christ had taken my place, becoming my substitute, my scapegoat for all the wrath of God that I deserved. I cast myself totally upon His mercy, convinced that His death and resurrection accomplished victory over the power of sin and death for all who will believe and receive Him. Still, I was extremely despondent and lacked any conscious sense of hope.

And then, one morning after awaking from sleep, I suddenly became aware that something was drastically different. It was as though a great weight and burden had been lifted off of me. It was unmistakable. Then, there came to me the glorious insight that Jesus Christ had set me free! It was truly a sovereign work of God, for no one else could ever even touch the pain or turmoil that I had experienced during those tormenting months. The Lord Jesus, with the same power with which He rose from the grave, set my life free—dramatically, yet tenderly—from its constant torments.

I can now boldly say from experience that Jesus is truly Who He claims to be: the only Way, the Lord Supreme, and the Head over all things. He stands forever as the source and dispenser of life as it was intended to be experienced.

Suffering Now Produces Glory Then—
Keep Your Eyes On THAT DAY So As Not To Fall Away

Since that time, it's not always been easy. To the contrary, I have often gone through some tough times, and life has had its ups and downs. After all, God has called us to be "overcomers," and it is a sobering reality that there is no overcoming without something to overcome. God's Spirit gives comfort, strength, and encouragement to us personally as well as through our brothers and sisters in the Lord. Our suffering is also eased and made more tolerable through our relationship with the Son of God Who entered into conflict with this temporal world order, defeating it and bringing to nothing its power. [John 16:33.] All who firmly cling to Him by remaining focused on Him and obedient to Him are empowered to walk in victory over all the works and deceits of the world, the flesh, and the devil.

One day, however, when we stand before God at The Judgment, I think we will probably wish that we had gone through even more trials, temptations, persecutions, and difficulties. Why? Because, though we may suffer today, perhaps even through our entire lives, our eternal reward will be proportionately phenomenal tomorrow. That is—the more we overcome, the greater our reward will be. And, compared to an eternity of eternal bliss with our Father, the longest and most difficult life here in this temporal realm is but a struggling breath. If we overcome the tests and temptations of the things we face *now* by drawing on the grace of God, He will richly reward us *then,* and (if even out of necessity) the more we draw on Him, the more we shall partake of Him.

As far as saying that the greater the hassles we go through in this present life, the greater the glory to be revealed in us in the life to come, isn't that what our brother Paul meant in 2 Corinthians 4:16-18? There, he encourages us not to give up or faint in the trials of this life as we look forward to the eternal rewards and joys that await us if we remain faithful to the Lord right now. He wrote, "...we do not become discouraged. We do not faint. Though outwardly we are wasting away, yet inwardly we are being renewed day by day. For our light, momentary affliction (this slight distress of the passing hour) *is producing for us* an eternal weight of glory beyond all comparison! So, we fix our eyes not on the things that are seen, but on the things that are unseen. For the things that we can see with our physical eyes are temporal (brief and fleeting), but the things that are unseen are eternal."

Also, if we are willing to suffer reproach and suffering from the world for turning from its ways to follow Jesus Christ, then we will reign with Him. Beyond comparison—with a treasure beyond measure—we will be rewarded "chief relief" for the "brief grief" we may suffer in this present life. If we suffer *for* Him, we will reign *with* Him. [2 Timothy 2:12.]

Sounds like an exchange far in our favor to me!

In Romans 8:1, he said, "...I consider that the sufferings of this present time (this present life) are not worth being compared with the glory that is about to be revealed to us, in us, for us, and conferred on us!" So, we see that as we keep our eyes set on the goal before us of being found settled in Him on that Great Day, this will help us through the difficulties of this present life. This is also precisely what our Lord did.

We know this from reading Hebrews 12:2, which exhorts us to "fix our eyes on Jesus, the Author and Perfecter of our faith, who for the joy set before Him endured the cross..." Notice that He was able to endure the cross because He had His gaze set on "the joy set before Him." This was ultimately His Father and His Father's will (and this, of course, included redeeming a people for God).

If we are to be overcomers, then, like our Lord, we also must maintain a Heavenly focus that is fixed on God and His kingdom. As Hebrews 12:2-3 informs us, we can find solace, comfort, and encouragement in the midst of suffering in this visible, temporary realm as we keep our eyes on Jesus and on the reward that awaits us in the coming manifestation of God's eternal kingdom.

It is obvious that our challenges can be made less daunting by keeping the thought before us that faithfulness to the Lord, especially through trial and suffering, will reap a bountiful harvest and reward in The Day Of Judgment, in particular, the reward of seeing on the Lord Jesus' face a unique expression of love, joy, and satisfaction that only the faithful will behold.—*So that life we don't despise, we must keep our eyes on the Prize!*—Jesus and the rewards of faithfulness to Him. For the greatest reward of all that is set before us is an eternal closeness of union and fellowship with God and our Savior, Jesus Christ. It is reserved for those who rise above their present circumstances through their focus on God and their pursuit of Him and His eternal realm. We are called to turn our focus away from present, temporal situations, fixing our gaze above on the Lord and the eternal, unseen things of His kingdom. [2 Corinthians 4:17-18; Hebrews 10:32-11:1.] The things that are visible and temporal shall not overcome those who genuinely and intensely seek and love the invisible, eternal things.

In the meantime, the expectation of reward *then* in exchange for suffering *now* does not mean that we should devise some kind of sadistic, self-induced pain and torment. Furthermore, although the Lord allows us to face severe tests, know that He is not cruel, sadistic, unreasonable, and overly demanding. He does not expect us to enjoy difficulties and trials in and of themselves. After all, that's why they are called "difficulties and trials!" But He is wanting us to understand that our praise and worship as well as our peace and joy are not to be diminished by anything whatsoever that we go through, whether it is tough or easy. Our focus is to remain fixed on Him, and our fulfillment must be found always and only in Him, not our circumstances. Circumstances change, but our God does not, and the more we are settled in Him, the less the fickled, fluctuating situations of this present life will affect us. In regards to holy living, the Holy Spirit is working in us to make us like our Father and our elder Brother, Jesus—steadfast and immovable, no matter what comes our way.

Personally, I know that I will forever be desperately in need of the Lord. Of a certainty, it is only His grace that keeps me in pursuit of Him. How weak I am, yet how merciful and powerful He is.

Though it is often painful, I am thankful that, on the anvil of my heart, the Father is forging the character of His Son in me. I know that all who refuse to deny Him and, instead, continue to walk faithfully obedient to His Spirit regardless of circumstances, He will bring through every trial to His eternal, glorious Presence with exceedingly great, overflowing joy.

So, glory to God! No wonder we read in James 1:2 to consider it pure *joy* whenever we encounter trials of any sort or fall into various temptations. If we overcome these threats to our kingdom walk, the Lord will bestow His grace and glory on us in a proportionate manner.

Hallelujah! As 1 Thessalonians 5:16-17 exhorts, we should "Be joyful always; pray continually; give thanks in *all* circumstances [*no matter what the circumstances are*, be thankful and *give thanks*], for this is God's will for [us] in Christ Jesus."

Spiritual Joy, Not Fleshly Happiness

I thank God that there are glorious, enjoyable, even fun times to be had in this present life as we walk with Him. However, I have realized that The Kingdom of God is not a walk in the park, and we are not to try to convince God to always make life "easy." I now know that He never intended for this present life in this fallen, sin-tainted realm to be primarily a bed of ease. In Luke 22:28, our Lord didn't refer even to His own ministry as full of frolicking happiness and leisure. Instead, He referred to His ministry as His "trials." Although, as Hebrews 1:9 tells us, He was "anointed with joy above his peers," He was, nonetheless, as Isaiah 53:3 declared, "a Man of sorrows, and acquainted with grief." This should teach us that we can be full of the fruit of the Spirit known as "joy" even when we don't feel happy. Joy is based on the solid reality of the unchanging God and His unshakable kingdom and the indwelling Presence of His Spirit in the life of a believer. On the other hand, happiness is based on the fickleness of fluctuating, human emotions and changing circumstances. In short, joy is a fruit of the Spirit; happiness is an emotion of the flesh.

Similarly, if we truly walk with Him, we will find ourselves also referring to this present life more as a time of trials than of ease. We will come to see that the "Gospel Ship" is a battleship, not a cruiseship, with "worship" being among the main weapons of our "warship."

God did not send His Son to suffer and die so that we can have our lusts, egos, and selfish longings catered to. The purpose of this present life is to prepare us for the life to come by emptying us of self-centeredness and selfishness, filling us to overflowing with the Spirit of Jesus and His great, immeasurable love. We are not to be in love with this present, passing world's allurements. We belong to a different realm above, unseen and eternal.

Non-Contaminating Containers

Part of the preparation for that realm involves us facing deep and sometimes even severe dealings within us by God's Holy Spirit. But, as we have seen, He does not put us through difficulties just to give us hard times. He has a definite goal of equipping us to be holy vessels who are consistently able to contain and carry His glory without any pride and without our contaminating our union with Him. This requires *much* transformation of our inner beings by the Spirit and the word of God. Demotion must precede promotion. God must bring us to the end of ourselves so that we can fully experience Him.

Knowing these things will help us to not get angry or disappointed with God when things don't seem to be going the way that we would like them to. For, even in the midst of pain and difficulties, if we call out on God to deliver us, many times, He will reply, "Not yet!" [It's as though we ask, "Is it soup, *yet???*" And He says, *"No!!!"*] What I'm getting at is that we are sometimes prone to try to use God to simply cater to what *we* perceive are our needs, and we tend to blame unpleasant circumstances on the devil. However, oftentimes, our need is not for deliverance from our circumstances, but from ourselves and our stubborn self-will. Also, often when we think that certain things (particularly difficult ones) are cruel works of the devil, they can actually be the loving dealings of a holy God Who is determined to transform our characters into that of Jesus Christ His beloved Son.

We can make it easier on ourselves if we will learn to rest in God's love, mercy, and kindness. He is able, willing, and trustworthy to see us through. He has said that we should stop fretting and sweating and start just letting Him fully have His way in us, believing that He is with us even in the tough times. Then we shall surely see and experience His glory and intimately come to know Him and the workings of His kingdom.

Aliens

We are strangers, sojourners, and aliens in this present world, just as 1 Peter 2:11-12 says. There we read, "Dear friends, I urge you, as aliens and strangers in the world, to abstain from sinful desires. They war against your soul. Live such good lives among those who do not know God that, though they accuse you of doing wrong, they may see your good deeds and glorify God on the Day He visits us."

The Lord has designed this present life to be the laboratory; the test; the Artist's workshop. Though it plays an important role in who we are and are becoming, it is not to be the focus and love of our hearts. The challenge and test of this present life is to perceive and pursue the Lord and His invisible, never ending kingdom in the midst of the visible, temporary world. Will we turn from the pains and pleasures of everything around us in the visible, temporal realm so that we can fully and forever reach out to the Lord and His invisible, eternal kingdom, or will we perish in the perishing of the passing pleasures and pride of the present?

As the Lord Jesus says in Luke 17:32, *"Remember Lot's wife!"* [See Genesis 18 and 19, particularly 19:15-26, for the tragic details of her disobedience and wrong focus that led to her demise.]

Growing Pains

Not everyone has to go through the kind of trauma that I did. Even so, it is through "growing pains" that both our natural and spiritual lives develop into maturity. As Hebrews 5:8 reveals, we learn obedience and develop spiritual maturity through the things that we suffer, just like the Son of God did. Oftentimes, our spiritual being—our eternal essence—is strengthened and matured through the pain of confrontations with Satan and his demons, other people, the circumstances of life, our own selves, and even God Himself. Acts 14:22 echoes this, saying: "It is through much tribulation that we enter the Kingdom of God." In the spiritual as well as the physical realm, the taste and thrill of victory is so much sweeter, more exciting, and more fulfilling the more fierce, intense, and challenging the conflict is.

Each one of us, knowing by faith that a crown of righteousness awaits the victors and reward beyond our comprehension awaits the overcomers, must endure every moment in this life:

1) like a good soldier whose only aim is to please his commanding officer;

2) like a hard working farmer who will enjoy the fruits of his labor; and

3) like a focused, resolute, disciplined athlete who lives a temperate, non-extravagant life in order to be fit to compete and win the prize set before him.

The spoils, rewards and prizes of earth fade and pass away, but all that is found in Jesus Christ that is reserved for those who overcome and win the race against selfishness, sin, and Satan will shine and endure forever. We are able to do all of this only as we live by the strength and vigor of God's Holy Spirit. [See 2 Timothy 2:3; 4:7-8; 1 Corinthians 2:9-10; Revelation 2:7, 11, 17, 26-29; 3:4-6, 12-13, 21-22.]

Through His sacrificial death and resurrection, Jesus Christ has already secured the victory over every enemy of Truth and Righteousness. But much of the enforcing of this victory is to be done by the Church so that God's people can grow in their knowledge of Him and be further developed in their preparation for ruling with Him.

Trouncing The Tempter's Terrible, Testing Tricks

All who are genuine, committed disciples of Jesus Christ need to know that this fact alone will not assure victory over Satan and sin. We must not only confess Christ and renounce the devil. We must also walk in obedience to Christ in our day to day lives, instantly responsive to Him. In other words, we must "walk the talk," not just "talk the walk." This is the only way for us constantly to experience the victory that Christ won on Calvary.

Though temptations may at first seem to be like sweet fruit, they eventually are discovered to be bitter and deadly morsels of death (let us not forget the "fruit" eaten by Adam and Eve). Satan is not playing games—he is out for blood. He has an agenda that includes at the top of his list the destruction of humanity, particularly those who are disciples of Jesus Christ.

I believe that the following prophetic dream helps to verify this. It should help to awaken us all to the seriousness of the battle in which we are engaged:

In this dream, a man of God was spoken to by a sharply dressed, gentlemanly-looking "man" with cold, steely eyes. With calm, determined resolution, he said to the follower of Christ Jesus, "Don't you know I live for the moment I can destroy you?" This so-called "gentleman" was neither gentle nor a man. Instead, he (or, rather, "it") was a demonic assassin— a "hit-man," if you will—assigned by the devil to destroy that follower of Christ.

Of a certainty, the enemy is intent on destroying all who love the Lord.

But we need not fear the enemy or any of his emissaries. Jesus Christ is our ever present help in a time of trouble and He is our constant victory. However, we must have His strategy in every encounter with our spiritual foes. Only moment to moment abiding in Christ and obedience to His leadings will secure our victory over the enemy every time.

As we walk in obedience to God, continuously being filled with His Spirit, we will abide in a place of victory over the enemy and our own fleshly weaknesses and tendencies. Therefore, walking in defeat or victory is our choice. Thankfully (as was briefly touched on earlier), as disciples of Jesus Christ, if we fall for some of Satan's lies, we can tear down his strongholds in our lives and have sweet fellowship restored with God. How? By turning back to God in genuine, lifestyle-changing repentance as we confess our sins to Him.

The Angels Are Stepping Aside

The Lord has said that at this time, in the unseen, spiritual realm, angelic hosts who were at the forefront of the conflict against the fallen angels are stepping aside to allow the Church to take the lead and frontline position in the warfare. They will help us, but we are to head up the battle with our eyes fastened on the Lord Jesus—our captain and commander in chief. We are to stand strong in the Lord and in the power of His might. If we first submit ourselves to God, we can resist the devil and he will flee from us.

[See Ephesians 6:10; James 4:7.] We will then also be able to triumph over the tendencies of our flesh. If to God we submit, flesh will flounder.

The overcomer, "the victorious fighter," shall be granted the priceless honor of sitting with Jesus Christ "on His throne"—a symbol of authority and co-rulership with Him—just as Jesus Christ, the Lamb and Lion, overcame and was granted the right to sit with His Father on His throne. [The Revelation 3:21.]

Just think, through union with the victorious Jesus Christ, those humble, bold, mighty, victorious warriors shall be blessed and honored with the privilege and responsibility of actually sharing in the reigning over creation with God Almighty. How incomprehensible this is! But, if we are to share in the Lord Jesus' victory, we must follow His example, setting our face determinedly, immovably, "like a flint," [Isaiah 50:4-7] towards our Father and His will. Facing the Father and His will are identical—we can't accept one without the other.

So be encouraged, warriors of God. Although we are weak and ineffectual apart from Jesus, in and through Him we are strong and victorious. How glorious to know that though battles are still being fought, the war has already been won by Him...

It is finished!!! [John 19:30.]

The next time we engage in conflict, let us rejoice because conflict is the pathway to greater heights in God *if* we respond to conflict according to God's will and by the enablement of His grace. Conflict will make us better or bitter; ready to be refired or retired, so to speak. As we stand in Jesus Christ's victory and enforce His overcoming, resurrection power over His enemies (beginning with our own selfishness), we are brought into a greater awareness of God and His kingdom.

To be overcomers, we must face the threats, taunts, and temptations of the enemy and overcome them. Triumphing over tests produces triumphant testimonies. Never forget *The Requirement For Victory:*

"You can't experience a victory unless you go through a battle."

15

God Is In It!

Trying Situations Produce Triumphant Saints

To be nice and friendly to certain people is not always easy. Some folks are just plain ornery (come to think about it—that's true of all of us from time to time, isn't it?). But we have cause to rejoice...

God, in His wisdom, uses unsavory circumstances and relationships to benefit us. Somehow, *God is in it*—no matter how difficult the situation may be that we are facing. We must not give in to frustration, bitterness, unforgiveness, wrath, rage, curses, doubt, and unbelief. Instead, we should see to it that we keep our vision full of the Lord and His eternal perspective (e.p.). Likewise, our hearts, minds, and mouths should constantly be full of His praises. Remember, regardless of the circumstance, *God is in it!* As it is written in Romans 8:28, "...we know that *in all things* God *works* for the good of those who love Him, who have been called according to His purpose."

Therefore, this means that *God is in it* when we encounter situations such as those describe in 1 Corinthians 11:19. There, we read, "No doubt there have to be differences among you to show which of you have God's approval."

This verse reminds me of the account of Korah's rebellion against Moses, recorded in Numbers 16. The Lord turned Korah's wicked situation into a means to show whom He had chosen to come near to Him to minister to Him. So, we see that even in the midst of strife and evil contention, the God of perfect peace, righteousness, and holiness is ultimately at work to advance His eternal purposes.

God uses tough times in this present life to drive His people to seek Him diligently. Then, He can more uninhibitedly work out His purposes and perfect His nature in them. We see this even in the life of our Lord. The difficult times He faced in His earthly life served a lofty purpose of helping to drive Him to seek God intensely and cry-out to Him. As it says in Hebrews 5:7, "In the days of His flesh (His physical life on earth), Jesus offered up prayers and petitions with loud, vehement cries and tears to God—the One Who could save Him from death..."

Granted, in the midst of trying times, we may grimace and have an inclination to be furious or harbor resentment against the circumstances and the ones hurting us. But we need to remember that we are not left to the whims of the devil and his people—*God is in it!*

He is not the source of wickedness, neither does He promote it. Nevertheless, He works in the midst of it to bring about good. He takes situations that Satan means for evil and torment and turns them around to actually become vehicles of blessings that foster peace and promote His perfect will of goodness.

Triumphant In Tragedy & Successful In Spite Of Suffering

Consider Job...

His name is nearly synonymous with suffering, particularly suffering that comes upon the righteous. We discover in the book of the Bible that bears his name that Satan himself was allowed by God to bring horribly devastating and difficult circumstances upon him. The only restriction the Lord put on the devil was that he had to spare Job's life. Other than that, Satan pretty much had a "heyday" in his wreaking havoc in Job's life—a veritable "open season" to inflict tragedy on him and to afflict him with pain. Job's situation was so difficult and deplorable that, in Job 2:9, even his wife counseled him to "curse God and die!" But Job would not renounce God. Though he expressed bitter sorrow, anguish, grief, frustration, and even anger as he considered his situation and what seemed to him to be a complete lapse of justice, he remained faithfully committed to God and to the hope of God's mercy, declaring in Job 13: 15 (in the midst of his sufferings), "Though He slay me, yet will I wait for and trust Him...."

Although Job was severely tested, God never forsook his servant. He gave him the grace to endure incredibly difficult and crushing circumstances. Otherwise, Job would have miserably failed the test instead of merely faltered in it.

By God's grace,

in the midst of the test, Job learned to enter God's rest,
and when the trial was over, he became most blest.

Yes, in the end, God was merciful to Job. Not only did He deliver Job from His distresses, but He also blessed Job far more than he had been before this tragic and disastrous period of his life.

After his ordeal, not only was Job physically blessed and his health restored. As wonderful as those things are, by far, the greatest blessings that Job received were not merely recompenses for having gone through what he did. They were realities actually born out of his having gone through the harrowing experiences. By the grace of God, rather than Job's tests merely taking from him, he actually took from them, receiving a clearer, deeper understanding of himself, his need for God, and of God Himself.

So, although Satan himself attacked Job and his family, *God was in it.* All the while, the Lord was working out His eternal purposes and even bringing forth blessings in and through the very schemes and murderous plots of Satan.

Another example of God turning "Lucifer's lemons into lemonade" is when God allowed evil to touch His servant Joseph but did not allow it to destroy him. Joseph went through extremely terrible times of bitter harshness and unfair treatment for a large portion of his life. We read the main account about Joseph in Genesis 37-50.

Joseph's older brothers hated him so viciously and violently that they even plotted his murder. At the last minute, instead of killing him, they decided to sell him into slavery to a caravan of traveling merchants. The merchants then took him to Egypt—far from the places and people he knew and loved. In Egypt, he was again sold as a slave to Potiphar, one of Pharaoh's officials. While in the service of Potiphar, Joseph consistently refused the sexual advances of Potiphar's wife because Joseph loved the Lord and did not want to sin against Him. Ultimately, after Joseph again refused to give in to her lustful advances, she falsely accused him of attempting to rape her. Her lie caused Joseph to be unjustly thrown into a cruel, tough, Egyptian jail. There he remained for at least several years. However, God was with Joseph. Even in Joseph's darkest hour, *God was in it!*

The Scriptures reveal that the Lord was working in the midst of these potentially crippling, devastating, and tragic events. Genesis 39:21 says that even when Joseph was in captivity, *"...the Lord was with him;* He showed him kindness and granted him favor..."

After Joseph endured unfair humiliation and suffering for many years, the Lord suddenly and miraculously changed his condition. The change was drastic to say the least, for overnight Joseph exchanged the prison for the throne. He became one of the mightiest men on earth—even a prime minister or co-regent, second only to the Pharaoh in what had been the land of his captivity. His land of humiliation became his land of exaltation. In his exalted position, he was used by the Lord to save multitudes from starvation, including his brothers who had originally sent him on his trek through tribulations...

Due to the worldwide famine that occurred in those days, Joseph's brothers came to Egypt seeking food. Although they did not immediately recognize Joseph, he clearly recognized them. However, even after all of the cruelties that Joseph endured due to the wickedness of his elder brothers, he forgave them, telling them that *God was in it!*

In Genesis 45:5-8 and in chapter 50, verse 20, we discover Joseph's wise insight into the circumstances of his life. After revealing to his brothers that he was their brother, they cowered before him in fear. But he said, "...do not be distressed and do not be angry with yourselves for selling me here, because it was to save lives that *God sent me ahead of you*...to preserve for you a remnant on earth and to save your lives by a great deliverance...You intended to harm me, but *God intended it for good* to accomplish what is now being done, the saving of many lives. So now *it was not you who sent me here, but God..."*

Yes, *God was in it!* He was right in the midst of Joseph's horrific ordeals, terrible tragedies, trials, and temptations. Know that God has no "blind side." He was not playing "catch-up" with the devil. The enemy did not sneak up on the Lord and "pull something over" on Him in regards to Joseph. To the contrary, God was in the situation from the beginning, quietly working out His perfect, loving will even through the wickedness of Joseph's brothers...

What an almighty God we serve! Through His limitless power and wisdom, the holy God—in Whom there is no darkness [see 1 John 1:5]—can use evil and its spiritual darkness, hatred, and even death to ultimately further His own ways of holiness, light, love, and life. Though it might not have seemed this way when Joseph was in captivity, there is no such thing as "the wastefulness of God." Not a single moment of his life was wasted—not even the darkest, most unfair, and wicked—because God used them as tools to mold and shape Joseph's character and to prepare him to overcome future tests.

As with all of God's *faithful* saints, Romans 8:28 was fulfilled in Joseph's life. God made *all* things work together and fit into a plan for good for Joseph because Joseph loved Him and was called according to His design and purpose. These things included not only those that most people call "good," but also things that the majority of people consider "evil."

Joseph's life was a classic example of God's often repeated, threefold pattern for dealing with His people: first the giving of a vision, then the testing of the vision, then the fulfilling of the vision. Or, we could say it this way: first the birth of the vision, then the death of the vision (or so it seems to us. However, perhaps a better way to state this part of the process is that we must "relinquish" the vision to the Lord lest we make an idol of even this vision from God, and also to teach us to depend on Him for the fulfillment of whatever He plants within us), then follows the seeming resurrection of the vision, and then its fulfillment.

As Psalm 105:19 reveals, until what Joseph had prophesied would happen actually occurred, *the word of the Lord* (not the devil) tried and tested him. Joseph grew spiritually strong in the midst of the difficulties he faced in life. Not only was his faith and his love for God deepened, but, as we have mentioned, he was also equipped to masterfully handle the tests and responsibilities he would face in the future.

Another example of potential tragedy turning into triumph is the story of David, the king of Israel.

Chapters eighteen through twenty-six of First Samuel contain various accounts of King Saul's futile but earnest attempts to kill David, even though David had served Saul faithfully and had been promised by the Lord that he would be king. Because of the insane jealousy and dangerous wrath of King Saul, David often fled for his life.

1 Samuel 24:1-3 even contains an account of an occasion when David—the mighty warrior—had to quietly wait as Saul used the bathroom in a cave where David and his men were hiding. This was probably somewhat humiliating for David, the great military leader. But no matter what David faced—*God was in it!*

In the midst of his ordeals, David learned that he could confidently trust in the Lord and depend completely on Him. While on the run *from* Saul, David was running hard *to* the Lord. Through David's many, difficult trials—even as a lowly servant on the run from his insane master—God made him into a king fit and wise enough to rule over Israel.

In David's faithfulness to God in demotion and humiliation, he was proven trustworthy to handle promotion and exaltation. His trusting *in* the Lord preceded and led to his being trusted *by* the Lord—serving preceded being served, obeying came before ruling, running *from* a man came before reigning *over* many men, testing led to resting, tragedy came before triumph, and trials preceded the throne.

Moses also faced difficulties, unfairness, and rejection. So did Noah, Elijah, our Lord Jesus, and every other saint throughout history. As Paul said in Acts 14:22, "...it is through many hardships and tribulations we must enter the Kingdom of God." Yet, in spite of what they faced, *God was in it.* Their lives testify of God's faithfulness, grace, and triumphant love that are ever at work— even in the midst of terrible, seemingly unchecked wickedness.

God is in it, allowing wickedness to go no further than His eternal and perfect purposes will allow. As it is with all those who seek God, difficult circumstances and difficult people are tools used by His Spirit to mold us into vessels who have the glorious, holy nature of the Lord worked *in* us for display and demonstration *through* us.

Be assured that God is not playing "catch-up" with the devil. He is not running around after the enemy, trying to patch up and fix all of the destruction, pain, and chaos that he engineers behind God's back.

No way.

Satan *never* catches God unawares. He *never* gets away with *anything*. He may win some battles, but he is defeated in the war. Although at times it looks as though the exact opposite is true, Satan *never* ultimately wins.

To the contrary, God strengthens us with the very things Satan used to try to destroy us. This drives Satan nuts! How it frustrates him and his legions to see God at work even in the midst of the most demonic situations. The Lord works with what they intended to be stumbling stones that cast us down and destroy us. He turns them into stepping stones whereby we are drawn nearer to Him, deeper in His love, higher in His Spirit, and equipped with more strength and victory than before.

As we have noted in the previous chapter, difficulties will cause us to become either better or bitter—the choice is up to us. Will we be self-centered and demand our supposed "rights" to be loved and respected? Or, will we acknowledge and confess that, when we came to Jesus, we died (which included dying to all of our ways and so-called "rights")? Our Lord now holds the reins of our lives. We are to always remain subject to God, trusting Him in His love, wisdom, and sovereignty to use whatever He deems necessary to mold and make us into vessels of honor who are able and willing to fully complete His will and thus reveal His untainted glory.

Such insight does not make us mere pawns in the devil's hands. We are not left to blow like leaves in the winds of chance. We are not called to be "wusses" who have no backbone or willingness to fight. But if something comes our way that we are to deal with "head on"—with vigorous resistance—the Lord will lead us as to what we are to do. We are to keep our focus on God and our hearts always at rest in Him as we *respond* to Him, not merely *react* to circumstances.

Scalpels, Pearls, And Diamonds

God can turn around even the most trying times and make even the most difficult people we encounter to ultimately be sources of blessings.

Whether it comes from difficult circumstances or difficult people, a trial or test is like a scalpel. It has the ability to inflict great pain and discomfort on the body and can even cause death. However, in the hands of a skillful surgeon, though still inflicting some temporary pain, it can be an instrument of healing, deliverance, and life—curing caused by cutting is often the result of a surgeon's scalpel.

As I consider the trials that saints must go through in order to attain a mature Christian character, I am reminded of the pearl. A pearl is produced from a grain of sand that enters an oyster shell, causing great discomfort to the oyster. In an attempt to relieve its torments and suffering, the oyster secretes a substance to surround and coat the grain of sand. After much pressure and a great deal of time, a beautiful and rare pearl is formed—beauty born of bother is a pearl born of pain.

A diamond is formed in a similar way. Deep in the earth, subjected to intense heat and pressures for a prolonged period of time, common coal goes through incredible, totally transforming changes, producing the treasured diamond—preciousness produced by pressure is a diamond developed during distress. And, even after forming, the diamond's worth is increased exponentially after it has been mined, cleaned, cut, and polished in the hands of a master gem cutter. It is then that its true value can be determined and when it can most radiantly and perfectly interact with light.

Sound familiar, saint?

Pain, irritations, heat, pressure, and long periods of waiting—they don't sound very appealing, do they? Nevertheless, they work together to produce healing and rare, wonderful, exquisite treasures.

Our characters are developed in much the same way as a pearl and a diamond. For, even as they are born of triumphing over trying traumas, spiritual and emotional darkness, heat, intense pressures, and lengthy times of solitude and/or difficulties work together to produce and develop the character of Christ within us.

Spiritual Genetics

Our spiritual genetics have been corrupted, leaving our spirits and minds corrupt and diseased. This condition has prevented us from dwelling on thoughts from God that are conducive to holistic health and the Presence of God. The prognosis for the human condition would be bleak (even "terminal") but for an intervening operation performed by "The Great Physician."

Spiritually speaking, we must "go under the knife"—allowing an "exploratory" by the Holy Spirit and the "x-ray" of God's Word to expose our deplorable state and deadly spiritual "disease" of sin. Then, we must allow the skillful hands of "the Holy Surgeon" to work deep within us. His intervening "surgery" can remove the spiritually cancerous condition of sin, cleanse our "hearts of hardening" towards God, and rid our minds of a cloudy fog of filthy, dark imaginings that have been passed down through our ancestors.

The Pains That Bring Gains

What will we do when irritations beset us? Will we react to difficult situations in fleshly anger, or respond to God with the wisdom of His Holy Spirit? Always remember that the Lord is desirous to transform us in the midst of our difficulties. He is far more intent on working something holy, eternal, and unshakable in us while we are in difficulties and even unholy situations than in getting us out of them. After all, the work wrought within us will last forever, yet the pain and the painful circumstances that produce the work shall soon forever pass away—even from memory. [See Isaiah 65:17, also The Revelation 21:4.] In short, God is more interested in getting the problem out of us rather than getting us out of the problem.

This concept is revealed in His saving us from the penalty of sin, yet leaving us subject to the presence of sin with the intention of utilizing the greater power of His Holy Spirit to enable us to overcome the power and, therefore, the practice of sin. In other words, His purpose is to get the world out of us rather than get us out of the world. As our Lord prayed in John 17:15, "I do not pray that You take them out of the world, but that You keep them from its evil [or the evil one.]"

Insulated. Not isolated.

The wounds you may have; the physical, mental, emotional, and/or spiritual rapes that you have endured; the lack of self-worth;

the gut-wrenching pain; the traumas you have tasted; the gaping holes in your soul; the depression and defeats that have held you fast and threatened to pull you beneath a murky bog of despair; your inability to cry or to stop crying; the fears you have faced and may yet still face; the anguish and anger you have felt and that may drive you even now; the thoughts that are but the tormenting screams and taunts of demons; the chasm of emptiness within that you have tried so many times to fill, but to no avail—all of these are areas in which the glory of God can be uniquely and manifestly revealed.

Know that you have not been allowed to be torn without God intending to bind you up. Nothing has touched you that He has not first felt. God also longs to reveal Himself, His love, and His acceptance to you in every area of your heart and mind where all you have known is shame or rejection.

The devil may have attacked you fiercely, but God has purposed to use the devil's worst against you to perfect His best in you. God has allowed Satan limited access to you in the knowledge that, as you yield yourself fully and consistently to the Holy Spirit, He will glorify Jesus most in the very areas of your life where you were most wounded. He will also use you to help others overcome in the same areas of struggle and pain in which you have overcome.

Your deep needs are like river beds or lake beds that have not been dug in vain. Your inner being has not been excavated and evacuated—torn up—to just leave you feeling empty and without purpose. God desires to fill you in the areas of your deepest need and pain with the healing, flowing waters of His Holy Spirit.

The day can actually arrive in which you rejoice that you were born into that abusive, harsh, or negligent family; where you can wholeheartedly praise the Lord for the husband or wife that mistreated you, cheated on you, and/or rejected you; where you can sincerely thank God for all who have abandoned you and hurt you; where you can wholeheartedly bless those who have cursed you; do good to those who have mistreated and despitefully used you; give to those who stole from you; honestly love those you hate you; and offer your life for those who would readily hurt, maim, destroy, and even kill you and those closest to your heart. You can come to the place where, without a warped sense of self-deprecation, you sincerely and joyfully glorify God and actually thank Him for suffering and all your trials, whether physically, mentally, emotionally, or spiritually.

How???

By your opening up to God and allowing Him total access to every part of your being—the good, the bad, the happy, the sad, all zeal, all indifference, all gain, all loss, the pain, the wounded, the warped, the perverted, the beautiful, and the ugly—you prepare the way for Him and His healing nature to be revealed in your pain and woundedness. Let Him have his way in and through you, and ask Him to do everything He desires all around you. Let Him expose, explore, and heal. Hold nothing back. Give Him *everything*. Tell Him *all* of your concerns, thoughts, feelings, and fears. Be open with Him and He will be open with you; try to hide and you'll not find Him.

Meditate on the fact that rough and tough times are often catalysts that drive us to God. Very often, they are intended to break down our self-sufficiency and wrong focus and to cause us to set our hearts and minds on things above. This is not to say that Satan is not an enemy who we will sometimes have to put in his defeated place as we enforce the victory of Christ. But know that the Spirit of the Lord even sometimes uses the devil to work out God's ultimate purposes for us...

Satan Defeated, Yet Used

For example, though the Scripture is clear that Satan is defeated and that he will flee from us if we resist him after first submitting to God, even Paul the apostle faced daunting opposition from Satan. He even prevented Paul from visiting certain saints when Paul intended to do so. {See John 12:31; 16:11; Colossians 2:13-15; James 4:7; and 1 Thessalonians 2:18.}

And, although Satan is defeated through the finished work of Christ on the cross and in the resurrection, in The Revelation 2:10-11, the risen Lord told a certain assembly of saints, "Do not be afraid of what you are about to suffer. I tell you, the devil will put some of you in prison to test you, and you will suffer persecution for ten days. Be faithful, even to the point of death, and I will give you the crown of life. He who has ears, let him hear what the Spirit says to the assemblies (the gatherings of the saints). He who overcomes (is victorious) shall in no way be injured by the second death."

Notice that our Lord did not tell the saints at that time to resist the devil and he would flee from them. To the contrary, He warned them of imprisonment that would come directly from the hand of Satan. Was the Lord abdicating His victorious place as Head over all creation to Whom all things are now made subject and to Whom all power on earth and in Heaven has been given?

No way.

Instead, He was revealing that He in His unchallengeable might has the right and ability to even use Satan—the archenemy of God and good—as an instrument to further God's eternal, perfect plans.

Oh, how this frustrates and infuriates Satan!

Be Led By Our Head

This means, therefore, that we cannot just take a Scripture and "claim it" or "use it" at our discretion—we must follow the leadings of God's Holy Spirit (Who will always speak what He hears from Jesus, will glorify Him, and will testify about Him and His overwhelming victory over self, Satan, and sin). But, believe me, the saints the Lord was speaking to in The Revelation passage we just read could have hollered themselves hoarse rebuking the devil and quoting Scriptures at him concerning his defeat, but this would not have kept them out of prison and the rest of their fiery ordeal!

Why?

Because the Lord Jesus—the Lord of all—had already spoken what would happen. Thus, we must always keep our eyes set on the Lord, not the circumstances in which we find ourselves. Also, we must keep our ears open to His perfect leading of His perfect will, not to our interpretations and so-called "Scriptural" dogma.

Keep in mind the following enlightening verses as you face the "stuff" of life:

2 Corinthians 4:11, "For we who live are *constantly being handed over to death* for Jesus' sake, so that *His life* may be revealed in our mortal body...

Ephesians 5:19-20, "Speak out to one another in psalms and hymns and spiritual songs, offering praise with voices and instruments and making melody with all your heart to the Lord, *at all times and for everything giving thanks* in the name of our Lord Jesus Christ to God the Father."

Remember 1 Thessalonians 5:16-17, which we looked at in a previous chapter, "Be joyful always; pray continually; give thanks in *all* circumstances [*no matter what the circumstances may be,* be thankful and *give thanks*], for this is God's will for you in Christ Jesus."

1 Peter 2: 20-21, "What kind of glory is there in it if, when you do wrong and are punished for it, you take it patiently? But *if you bear patiently with suffering which results when you do right and that is undeserved, it is acceptable, pleasing, and commendable before God* (finding favor with Him). *For even to this you were called—it is inseparable from you vocation).* For *Christ also suffered* for you, leaving you His personal example, that you should *follow in His footsteps."*

1 Peter 3:9, 14-15a, and 17, "Do not repay evil with evil or insult with insult, but with blessing, because *to this you were called so that may inherit a blessing...even if you should suffer for what is right, you are blessed.* Do not fear what they fear; do not be frightened. But in your hearts set apart Christ as Lord...It is better, *if it is God's will, to suffer* for doing good than for doing evil."

1 Peter 4:1-2, "Therefore, *since Christ suffered in His body, arm yourselves also with the same attitude,* because *he who has suffered in the flesh (in the body) has ceased from sin* (is done with intentional sin; has stopped pleasing himself and the world, and pleases God). As a result, he does not live the rest of his earthly life for evil human desires, but rather for the will of God."

1 Peter 4: 12-14, "Dear friends, do not be surprised at the painful trial you are suffering, as though something strange were happening to you. But *rejoice that you participate in the sufferings of Christ, so that you may be overjoyed when His glory is revealed. If you are insulted because of the name of Christ, you are blessed, for the Spirit of glory and of God rest on you."*

1 Peter 5:10 and 11, "And the God of all grace, Who has called you to His eternal glory in Christ, *after you have suffered a little while,* will Himself restore you and make you strong, firm, and steadfast. To Him be the power for ever and ever. Amen."

Remember the glorious command of Philippians 4:4, "Rejoice in the Lord *always*. I will say it again: *Rejoice!*"

And let us also not forget these instructions from James 1:2-4 and 12, *"Consider it pure joy...*whenever you are enveloped in or encounter *trials of any sort* or fall into *various temptations,* because you know that the testing of your faith develops perseverance. Perseverance must finish its work so that you may be mature and complete, lacking in nothing...*Blessed is the man who perseveres and is patient under trial and stands up under temptation,* for *when he has stood the test and been approved,* he will receive the victor's crown of life which God has promised to those who *love* Him."

Concerning such things, we have numerous promises of relief and blessing from God. Among them are:

Romans 16:20, "The God of all peace will soon crush Satan under your feet." In the meantime, as we have covered, God utilizes the devil as He will.

And how glorious is Romans 8:18(!): "I consider that the sufferings of this present time (this present life) are n*ot worth being compared* with the glory that is about to be revealed to us and in us and for us and conferred on us!"

Always keep in mind 2 Corinthians 4:16-18 (wonderful verses concerning e.p. (eternal *p*erspective), "...we do not lose heart. Though outwardly we are wasting away, yet inwardly we are being renewed day by day. For our light and momentary troubles (this slight distress of the passing hour) is ever more and more abundantly preparing and *producing and achieving* for us an everlasting *weight of glory* beyond *all* measure, excessively surpassing *all* comparisons and *all* calculations, a vast and *transcendent* glory and blessedness never to cease! Since *we consider and look not to the things that are seen but are unseen;* for the things that are visible are temporal (brief and fleeting), but the things that are invisible are deathless and everlasting."

God has not given us over to whimsical winds of fate or the diabolical will of Satan. However, our all-wise, all-powerful God receives glory before a watching, learning creation as He utilizes the most base and wicked of circumstances and things to work out His most holy and sublime purposes. Furthermore, as we have seen, as we train ourselves to remain focused on God and full of His praises, regardless of our circumstances: He is pleased; His Spirit rests on us; we show ourselves approved as trustworthy servants, sons, and friends of the Lord; at times we engage in warfare against satanic foes; and we secure a sure blessing in the future beyond any comparison to all the problems and difficulties that we currently face.

Glory to God, the temporary pain is working eternal gain!!!

Choose The Choice To Change

We are called to be faithful to God, responding to every circumstance according to His will—always rejoicing in Him and praising his name—regardless of what we are facing, knowing that He is always in control.

Will we submit ourselves into the hands of The Great Physician, trusting Him to use the scalpel of the circumstances of life to do a work in us that leads to life, not death? Will we let Him have His way? Or will we refuse His expertise? Will we demand that He work on us according to our dictates? If so, we will find our "condition" growing steadily worse.

Like the oyster who secretes a substance to envelope an invading irritant, will we "secrete" the sweet nature of Christ to envelope the irritations of life, using them as catalysts to develop the rare, priceless treasure of His nature within us? Or will we just become irritated at the irritant, taking on its characteristics of grating, irritating hardness, thereby allowing it to have power over us, and thus never allowing Christ to be formed in us?

Similar to coal that is changed into a diamond, will we allow prolonged times of heat and pressure to transform us into treasures of God that are valuable, rare, beautiful, and able to display the glories of Him Whom 1 John 1:5 tells us is "light"? Or will we fuss and fume, full of doubt and gloom, and curse the dirt and darkness that surround us rather than yield to God? Will we allow the pain, filth, and spiritual deadness of our surroundings and our past to keep our hearts hardened and darkened? Will we cling to frustration and bitterness, thereby remaining like a common piece of dirty coal and making ourselves nearly insignificant as far as the Kingdom of God is concerned?

The choice is up to us...

Oh, that we would allow the Holy Spirit to complete the work that He is doing within us through our submissive and obedient responses to God, regardless of what we encounter or endure! May we be willing to allow the love of God to be revealed to us and unveil the riches of His grace that He has already and permanently placed within us. The resultant image of Christ to which even just one of us will be conformed is infinitely more precious and valuable than all the pearls and diamonds in creation.

We need to always keep in mind the truth of Ephesians 6:12. There we discover that we combat evil spiritual beings who work through people. Such struggles cause us grief and misery. However, knowing that our real warfare is with fallen spirits instead of the human beings they use helps us to keep our hearts right—free from hatred and proud judgments against other people. Knowing who we are really struggling against also helps us to focus our energies on fighting our real, spiritual enemies rather than the physical vessels and vassals through whom they work.

As we've seen, we can rejoice even in the midst of the most intense demonic attacks, for even then, the Lord does a work that benefits us—*God is in it.* He is ever working out His sovereign, perfect, and beautiful will, not only through acts of kindness expressed by those who follow His Spirit and desire to bless us, but also even through evil actions of ornery, difficult, demonically driven people who delight in tormenting us.

Judgment Day is coming, and all who will be found faithful to God—those who are perceiving and pursuing Him and His eternal realm in the midst of this temporary, sometimes difficult, swiftly fleeting life—shall find themselves greatly rewarded beyond comprehension. Even in the most evil of times, as we yield to God's Spirit and walk in His ways through dependency on Him, God works His nature into us, His Spirit rests mightily on us, and we increase our glorious reward in Heaven.

On the other hand, those who are tools of Satan in this life shall discover that they are actually his fools. They shall suffer the same unutterably horrible and terrifying condemnation as their hero—everlasting suffering and damnation because of pride that led to selfish, rebellious defiance of God. Having chosen to live independently of God in this brief life of preparation, they shall reap what they have sown and will therefore be forever cutoff from Him and suffer eternal damnation.

May we always remember that things that appear to be good can in fact not be good for us (not all things that seem to be "good" are "of God"—a good thing is not necessarily a "God thing"). Similarly, things that appear to be bad (such as circumstances that are extremely painful and difficult) can actually be blessings in disguise (or at least be doors or pathways that lead to blessings).

Therefore, let's live with no fret or spiritual sweat as we simply let God have His way by maintaining our hearts' and minds' focus on Jesus. Rather than give into despondency, judgment, bitterness, anger, resentment, and/or retaliation, let us keep our eyes on the Lord, be thankful to Him in all things, and bless those who curse us, do good to those who despitefully use us, and pray for those who mistreat us. To the degree that we cam be thankful and joyful no matter what we face, to that degree we experience victory.

Therefore, no matter what we go through—whether easy or difficult, or even righteous or wicked—we can rest and rejoice in our Lord, knowing that *God Is In It—Trying Situations Produce Triumphant Saints!*

16

God's "Psychology"

From Night To Light—Pain To Gain

There is a revelation that brings pain, yet leads to a transformation that brings gain.

Psalm 16:11 tells us that in God's Presence is fullness of joy. Before we break forth with inexpressible joy, however, we may endure times of inexpressible sorrow as we experience a revelation of our personal lack of godliness and purity of heart. At some point(s) in life, after confronting the Lord in a new, intimate way, most saints have confessed to Him something similar to the famous declaration of Job 42:5-6: "I have heard of You by the hearing of the ear, but now my eye sees You. Therefore I abhor myself and repent in dust and ashes."

In Isaiah 6:1-5, we read of a time the prophet Isaiah saw the Lord sitting on His heavenly throne. When this happened, Isaiah didn't break forth in happy song and a joyous "Whoopee!" Instead, he cried out, "Woe is me!" Great terror and grief came upon him because of conviction for sin. This conviction occurred as his personal weaknesses were clearly revealed to him in the light of God's manifested holiness and glory.

Such is the nature of light—

It exposes.

It reveals.

It brings out into the open
that which was hidden in darkness and secrecy.

And, as 1 John 1:5 reveals, God *is* light. By His Spirit and the illumination of His Word, God exposes our inner beings and motives, showing us what they truly are. Instead of reveling in darkness, we are to reveal light and walk in the purity of the Lord.

One of the principles of God's kingdom is that He *exposes* sin so that He might *depose* it and *dispose* of it because He does not forcefully want to *impose* what He *proposes*. Therefore, when the God Who is light unveils our innermost recesses, any darkness within us should be confessed, renounced, and forsaken. This exposing and cleansing is almost never a pleasant experience, but it is a necessary one if we desire to grow into maturity in Jesus Christ—God does bring pain, but such pain leads to gain.

This is one of the main reasons why many choose to remain in the "vicinity" of His Presence—hanging around with others who profess the Lord—but will not open themselves fully to Him. They would rather hide—chained and unchanged—in darkness than face the exposure, liberation, and transformation that awaits them in God's light.

How sad.

Psalm 36:9 tells us that only in *His* light will we see light. We will be able to receive light only as we are willing to forsake any darkness within us that He exposes. This deep, inner searching by the Spirit of God reveals dense darkness, hidden agendas, petty selfishness, and a love and a cry for mere material creature comforts.

The God Of Light, Protection, And Peace Uses Darkness, Fire, And Tempests

The Living God dwells in unapproachable light [1 Timothy 6:16; 1 John 1:7]. In fact, as we've already mentioned, 1 John 1:5 reveals that He even *is* light and in Him is no darkness whatsoever. However, an enveloping cloak of darkness often precedes a revelation of God and the intense light in which He dwells.

As examples, consider the following:

Romans 4:16 reveals that Abram (whom God later named "Abraham") figuratively became the father—the predecessor and forerunner—of those who live by faith. In Genesis 15:12, we discover that when God made covenant with Abram and drew near to finalize the agreement with the man of faith, a deep *darkness* and great terror came upon Abram.

Isaiah 45:15 states that the Lord is a God Who hides Himself. In 1 Kings 8:12 and 2 Chronicles 6:1, Solomon reveals that the Lord's hiding place is "...in the thick *darkness.*" Psalm 18:11 tells us that God has made *darkness* His secret place, and His canopy that is around Him is *dark* waters and *thick clouds* of the skies.

When the nation of Israel met with God the first time at Mount Sinai, they "...came near and stood at the foot of the mountain; and the mountain burned with fire to the very heart of the heavens, with *black clouds and deep darkness.* And the Lord spoke...out of the midst of *the fire.*" [From Deuteronomy 4:11 and 12. Also see 5:22 and Hebrews 12:18.]

Notice that He spoke from the midst of the fire. Similarly, Psalm 50:3-4 says, "Our God comes, and does not keep silence, a fire devours before Him, and round about Him a mighty tempest rages." Interestingly, both fire and darkness are again mentioned together, surrounding the Lord. Often, when it seems as though we are going to "fry" in fiery, dark trials in which we find ourselves, we are on the threshold of new and fresh revelation from our God of light Who speaks to His people while He is surrounded by black clouds, thick darkness, and from the midst of fire. In fact, according to Hebrews 12:18-29 and Isaiah 33:14 He Himself is "a consuming fire" and "everlasting burnings." Furthermore, when we find ourselves in a thick, black, raging tempest, we need to remind ourselves of the fact that fire, tempests, and darkness are often the last "cloaks" covering an unprecedented revelation of God to us.

From the preceding Scriptures, we learn that the God of light uses darkness, fire, and/or tempests as (1) tests, as (2) a source of blessing, (3) an object lesson, and (4) as a preparation for ministry:

(1) He uses trying times as tests to see if we really desire to know Him, regardless of the costs. He also uses them to strengthen our hearts, deepen the roots of our belief in the unseen realm, and test us to see if we truly have faith. That is, He wants to see and show us whether we will persevere in our perception and pursuit of Him and His invisible kingdom of light, protection, and peace even when we are enveloped in spiritual darkness and fiery tempests in the visible, temporary realm. We grow in maturity as we recognize and overcome the distracting allurements of the visible realm. We are strengthened in our faith as we press through darkness, fire, and tempests for, by faith, we are aware that just

beyond these things, there awaits resplendently glorious, light-filled, comforting, and peaceful revelations and manifestations of our God.

(2) Isaiah 45:3 specifically states that darkness is used by the Lord as a source of blessing: "I will give you *the treasures of darkness,* riches stored in secret places..." These treasures and true riches of insight, depth of character, and eternal intimacy with Him are given "...so that you may know that I am the Lord, the God of Israel, Who summons you by name."

(3) God also uses darkness, fire, and a tempest as object lessons to teach us that we must not be moved by what we see, feel, or hear. For even the greatest glories, clearest insights, brightest light, most wonderful revelations, and even our God Himself are often hidden behind potentially deceiving and discouraging veils consisting of darkness, fire, and a tempest.

We are to do as 2 Corinthians 4:18 instructs us—look at the things that are not seen. When darkness tries to discourage us from the pursuit of an ever-deepening, intimate fellowship with God, we should choose to abide in the light by keeping our focus fixed on Jesus—the Light of the world [John 8:12], He Who is the Author and the Finisher of our faith. [Hebrews 12:2]. When we cannot sense or "see" Him, as it were, we must remind ourselves in the darkness of what He has revealed in the light. We are to walk in the light of His written word, which is a lamp for our feet. [Psalm 119:105.]

Furthermore, when we "feel the heat," we need to remind ourselves that God—the One known as a consuming fire—prepares us for His unveiled Presence by purging us of compromise and burning away what binds us in the fires of His holy love. And when we face the raging tempest, we need to meditate on the fact that in the arms of our Lord, there is perfect peace and rest, free from all threatening, contrary "winds" of adversity.

Will we choose to doubt in the darkness, "freak" in the fire, and totter and topple in the test of the tempest? If we do, our God will not forsake us, but neither will He be pleased with such responses. He calls to us to be strong in the power of His might in all these things, for He has determined that we shall not go down but through. Though He will not forsake us, He does not want to "sit in the mud" with us, so to speak. Instead, He wants us to cling to His Son, believing in His goodness, faithfulness, and call to us to sit with Him in Heavenly places, triumphant over *all* of the tests of this present life.

(4) In Matthew 10:27, the Lord again speaks of the benefits of us facing darkness. There He reveals that darkness is used by Him as preparation for ministry: "What I tell you *in the darkness,* speak in the light; and what you hear whispered in your ear, proclaim upon the housetops." When we go through dark, difficult times, our God does not forsake us. [Hebrews 13:5.] He may allow discomforting darkness and even distress and suffering for a time, but He is faithful to see us through and reward us for faithfulness to Him even when we were in the midst of temporary loss, distractions, and lusts.

He uses the difficult times as means of strengthening us, as 1 Peter 5:10 discloses, "...*after you have suffered for a little while,* the God of all grace, Who called you to His eternal glory in Christ, will Himself perfect, confirm, strengthen and establish you." By receiving comfort and strengthening from the Lord, we are equipped through experience, not just theory, to help others in a similar way. As 2 Corinthians 1:3-4 says, "Praise be to the God and Father of our Lord Jesus Christ, the Father of compassion and the God of all comfort, who comforts us in all our troubles, so that we can comfort those in any trouble with the comfort we ourselves have received from God." Also, in our moments of solitude with Him—times that are often marked by quietness and deep dealings of His Spirit within us—we receive insights and a transformation that benefit us as well as those to whom we shall proclaim His Truth. Most especially, we bring great joy to Him.

We also need to keep in mind that God is not merely hiding from us. To take this analogy further: He wants to "play," as it were, "hide-n-seek": He "hides" in the hope that we will "seek" for Him. To those who persist will be a reward beyond imagination of a revelation of the Lord that the casual passerby will never know. But don't be discouraged in your seeking. Rather, be encouraged, knowing that, according to Acts 17:24a and 26-28a,

"The God Who made the world and everything in it is the Lord of heaven and earth and does not live in temples built by hands and He is not served by human hands, as if He needed anything, because He Himself gives all men life and breath and everything else. From one man He made every nation of men, that they should inhabit the whole earth; and He determined the times set for them and the exact places where they should live. *God did this so that men would seek Him and perhaps reach our for Him and find Him, though He is not far from each one of us.* For in Him we live and move and have our being..."

Yes, be encouraged in your quest of finding God and, finding Him, plunging into His depths and forever searching Him out more.

It has been said that the darkest part of the night is just before the dawn. This should not discourage us. The night cannot stop the light, and the God Who is light and Who scatters the darkness is with us. Also, realize that shadows can exist only in the presence of light. The shadows that fall across your path may seem to subdue the light for awhile, but they do not utterly conquer it. The light shall prevail.

If we set our focus on clouds and on darkness, we will lose sight of Him Who is the Light (remember in Matthew 14:30 that Peter began to sink beneath the waves when he took his eyes off Jesus). Just as our Lord was with Peter in the midst of the storm, He is with us in the darkness, desiring that we keep our eyes on Him as we walk in His paths. That is how we will allow Him to see us through and bring us into a place of light where we perceive him more strongly and clearly than before our encounter with darkness.

Saints Are Surely Sitting With The Savior

Something that is worth noting here is the fact that those that are truly reborn of God's Spirit do not truly have to "get to God," as it were, for they are already "in" God, seated with Messiah Jesus His Son in Him in heavenly places. They need never fear that He will place something between them and Him through which they must struggle. However, He will sometimes allow us to go through times in which we *feel* that we are separated from Him and that we have to work through darkness, fire, and tempests. It tests us when we have to face times that lack the sort of feelings we often have in regards to spiritual matters, proving whether we have our hearts set on God *Himself* or on thoughts and feelings *about* Him. But again, remember that, in reality, He has already brought us to

Himself. Therefore, we must rest in His love, knowing that He is faithful and will never sever us from Himself.

Personal, Demonic, Or Divine Darkness, Fire, & Tempests?

One thing we should certainly not overlook as we consider these things is that not all encounters with darkness, devouring fire, and raging tempests are due to the Lord's dealings. For one thing, we may plunge ourselves headlong into such things or precipitate a gradual slide into their abysmal depths by our own self-will, stubbornness, pride, and disobedience to God. We must see to it that we walk and abide in the light by walking and abiding in the One Who is light; that we endure devouring fire by depending fully upon Him Who is a consuming fire; and that we ultimately come out unscathed by raging tempests by clinging to Him Who is our anchor and stability—truly, the Lord is the Rock Who doesn't roll, even in the midst of raging storms of fiery destruction and gloomy darkness. We can answer and fulfill such a call only by obeying the Lord through our total, trusting dependency on Him.

Our archenemy—Satan—delights in oppressing the people of God with thick, mental and emotional clouds of darkness, despair, doubts, depression, doom, and gloom. It requires discernment on our part to determine whether we should just wait on the Lord when we encounter trying times that appear dark to us, or whether we should enter into conflict with the devil and his angels.

There are times we should pray to God in submission to Him, and there are times when we should speak to Satan in resistance of him. Our Lord did both of these things...

> Hebrews 5:7 tells us that in the days of His flesh, the Son of God cried out to God with loud crying and tears. Yet, in Matthew 4:1-11, we have a record of Him rebuking the devil instead of praying to God.

Similarly, we are to maintain our rapport with God through prayer, yet also, by our wielding the Word of God—the sword of the Spirit—we are to also face the enemy and enforce his defeat that was secured by our Lord at Calvary and in His resurrection. [Colossians 2:15.]

God's dealings at this present time are remedial and upbuilding— He works with us and in us to transform us and to bring our character, vision, and pursuit into conformity with the image of His Son. On the other hand, John 10:10 reveals that the enemy's dealings with us are attacks intended to steal, kill, and destroy us without mercy.

When the Lord is increasing the revelation of Himself to us, rejoicing and glory will follow to the degree that we receive His light and walk in righteousness. [Remember, Psalm 119:130 tells us that the entrance of God's words brings light, and 1 John 1:5 even says that God Himself is light. If we refuse His word—whether through Scriptures, to us personally, or through others—we refuse His liberating, strengthening light from entering into us, *which is Himself.* Therefore, to reject God's words is to reject His light as well as God Himself.]

But, as John 3:16-22 makes clear, if we love the darkness, we will not want the true condition of our hearts to be made known. We will therefore run from the light because the things hidden in darkness are exposed in the light—shown for what they really are.

Ultimately, there is no escaping God's searching of our innermost beings. Before the end of time, The Revelation 20:11 reveals that even the earth and sky will flee, trying to hide from the awesome, revealing nature of God—the Judge of all—but there will be no hiding place. No one nor any thing is able to hide from the face of the Almighty—He Who is the Holy One and the one and only God. Everything is open and exposed to His all-seeing, all-searching eyes. As Hebrews 4:13 tells us, "...there is no creature hidden from His sight, but all things are naked and open to the eyes of Him to Whom we must give account." And Proverbs 15:3 states, "The eyes of the Lord are in every place, keeping watch on the evil and the good."

We should not futilely attempt to hide from God when He begins to expose our needs and weaknesses. On the contrary, we should run as fast as we can towards Him because He is our only hope.

The time is coming when our Lord will be revealed as the holy and just Judge. But, even so, know that the Judge is in love with you. We need not fear on that Day if we now everyday open to His Spirit and walk in obedience to His daily call to follow Him. His arms are opened wide and extended in love to us. Let us run to Him and embrace Him in childlike faith, trusting Him to receive us and help us.

Exposed—For Liberation, Not Condemnation

When our hearts are hiding nothing and inwardly things are visible and clear, we can move with confidence and boldness in our lives without fear of stumbling. Ephesians 5:13 says, "...when anything is exposed and reproved by the light, it is made visible and clear; and where everything is visible and clear there is light." On the other hand, if we attempt to hide things from ourselves and even God, whatever we try to hide will be the cause of a future stumbling and failing. We cling to darkness if we attempt to hide what we really are rather than honestly facing up to it and admitting it to ourselves and to others whom we trust.

It is important that we understand that God's deep dealings and searchings do not take place to condemn us or just to cause us some pain. No, God delights in us and loves us very much. 2 Peter 1:2-4 and Hebrews 12:10 reveal that He wants us to share in His nature and holiness so that we can fellowship forever with Him and participate in the realization of His eternal purposes.

But to be able to do so, we will have to allow Him to remove from us those things in us that displease Him, even though it may cause us some temporary discomfort and pain. As Hebrews 12:10-11 reveals, "Our fathers disciplined us for a little while as they thought best; but God disciplines us for our good, that we may share in His holiness. No discipline seems pleasant at the time, but painful. Later on, however, it produces a harvest of righteousness and peace for those who have been trained by it." Though God's dealings are sometimes uncomfortable, we need to remember that it is better to deal with the pain and cost of fixing a cavity today than to ignore it and have to deal with a root canal tomorrow.

Do you sense God dealing with you, perhaps even using darkness to expose darkness in you? Have you seen that, often, someone else's carnality triggers a carnal response in and from you?

Realize that no one has the power to make you yield to fleshly tendencies. They may be extremely carnal and fleshly, but, if you are God's child, you have no excuse to walk after the flesh. We must always and only walk after the Holy Spirit of God.

So, let God deal with you, even if He does so through darkness that hides your awareness of Him, or with a darkness from others that flushes out residual darkness in your own being. Just be certain to constantly yield your total self to Him. The Lord requires our cooperation in our process of maturing. We do this by living in complete and untainted honesty before Him, by agreeing with Him (which is the meaning of confession) when He reveals things in us that displease Him, and by turning from these things to cling to Him and His ways. It is stubbornly foolish and hurtful for us to choose to cling to anything that grieves the Holy Spirit or to try to hide anything from Him or ourselves. Remember that it is the fool who says no to God (this is one possible rendering of Psalm 53:1). And if it is the fool who says no, it is the wise it says yes.

As we are honest with God, ourselves, and others, as we allow the searchlight of the Holy Spirit to reveal all areas of darkness, and as we let go of everything that holds us back from complete devotion to God, we will bring joy to Him and will experience His delivering, liberating, transforming power. Then, walking free from the control of sin and darkness, we will be among the vessels of honor mentioned in 2 Timothy 2:21 who are totally devoted to God and His will, ready for Him to use as He desires.

When we think of being exposed, many would have the tendency to equivocate it with humiliation. However, if we live with openness before the Lord, we do not need to fear being publicly shamed and humiliated through Him exposing our weaknesses and personal struggles. This means that if we are willing to accept correction from the Holy Spirit and do something about it (that is, "repent"), we need not fear being embarrassed by someone "reading our mail" in the presence of others or "exposing and hanging out our dirty laundry," so to speak, for all to see.

If we live in openness and honesty before the Lord, He will not readily disclose our struggles to others, even if they be spiritually mature people. Any disclosure of our weaknesses would be granted to others only as a blessing to us and our spiritual growth. After all, the Lord delights in helping us in our weaknesses, not tearing us down. He does not mock us in our struggles and woundedness. As we read in Isaiah 42:3 as well as in Matthew 12:20, "A bruised reed He will not break, and a smoldering wick He will not snuff out…" Neither is He out to humiliate us. Isaiah 28:16 and Romans 9:33 tell us that "the one who trusts in Him shall not be put to shame."

Let's just not deceive ourselves by thinking we can bluff God. If we ever tried to do so, it would be us who were bluffed because, as we've already discussed, He sees all and knows all. [Hebrews 4:13.]

His Revealing, Not Our Digging (God-Dependency, Not Self or Co-Dependency)

This pattern of "being revealed that we may be healed" is truly "God's psychology." His forgiving, restoring blood, power, and love are abundantly available to us and are more than able to meet all of our needs if we will but face-up to the things that He reveals. Notice that I said "the things that *He* reveals," not things that we dig up and dredge up on our own (this would be a "work of the flesh" that would only strengthen the flesh, not help to subdue it" or "reckon it dead"—as we are exhorted to do in Romans 6:11). Although we are told in 1 Corinthians 11:31 to "judge ourselves so that we will not be judged," this is not granting license to sink into morbid introspection and religious self-examination. This only feeds our egos in a negative, unhealthy way.

Religious bondage is the heaviest chain one can wear. Assuredly, it is the most painful, deceptive, and destructive of chains, for it holds out an empty, lying promise and false hope of deliverance, all the while claiming to be speaking on behalf of the greatest and most holy Power in the universe—God Himself. It draws on a distant knowledge *about* God, yet does not have the spiritual substance that comes from relationship *with* God. Nonetheless, it talks loftily, speaks of heavenly things, and, often, it teaches about enjoying abundant life in this present world. However, it leaves its adherents poverty stricken and groveling in spiritual dirt for grub worms. These are, at best, the remnants of yesterday's spiritual "manna," so to speak.

At best, self-driven, self-deprecating pursuits of God, regardless of how "spiritual sounding" they may be, are only religious exercises in futility. They offer no enabling power or real spiritual substance, only rituals and non-empowering symbols.

If we desire to become closer to God and free from the dominion of sin, we must not turn our eyes on ourselves and on what *we* can accomplish. Otherwise, we just strengthen the cords and power of sin in us. Deliverance and victory are ours only as we keep our hearts and minds fixed and focused on Jesus, pursue Him diligently, and rely on Him to provide us with all we need to please Him fully.

As we turn away from the natural tendency to cling to past hurts and all of our selfishness and we choose instead to turn and cling to God, we find God's undeserved kindness, power, and peace filling us. Where there was hurt and pain, there is comfort. Where there were painful, bitter memories, there is the ability to forgive and to love. All of this is available to those who want to know Him intimately and are willing to stand in the truth, allowing God to reveal their darkness and replace it with His light, no matter how much it hurts or how great the cost. Believe me, the cost not to allow Him to do this will eventually be much greater and will result in much worse pain and torment, like having to deal with that root canal (or extraction—ouch!) because we ignored a toothache.

It may be slow going at times, but He will work within us as long as we are willing to do things and deal with things the way He chooses. After all, He's not our errand boy—He is God, and we had better learn to follow Him if we desire to experience Him and the fullness of His healing, delivering, transforming power.

Learning to release all *to* God, live totally *through* God, and remain focused only *on* God will set us free from the tyranny of both "self-dependency" and the "co-dependency." We are to be *God*-dependent, not *self*-dependent *or* *co*-dependent. And, as far as our brothers and sisters in Christ are concerned, we are to be *inter*dependent, not *in*dependent. Instead of remaining maimed, abused, wounded, and driven, we can become whole, healed, peaceful, and at rest. Also, through the Lord and our fellowship with our brothers and sisters in Christ, we are equipped to help others in distress.

The Path To Peace—"Inner Healing" God's Way

God certainly wants us to be set free from the torments and pains of our past. Many (probably most) people have gone through some "hellatious" times. Terrible traumas have rendered them deeply wounded and scarred in mind, emotions, and even body, threatening to destroy them. In Christ, however, we can enjoy complete freedom from the control, terror, and potential destruction of terrible events and painful memories, even those buried deep within us.

How?

Whenever we feel inner pain, we need to acknowledge it to God and, at times, to others whom we also trust. We shouldn't deny that we feel pain when we certainly do. We keep it in a healthy perspective by pouring out our hearts to the Lord all of our griefs, pains, disappointments, sorrows, hatred, pains, pleasures, sorrows, joys, and whatever else may be abiding or even brooding within our bosoms.

But, know that acknowledging pain does not mean we wallow in it and allow it to dominate and control our lives. It is one thing to bleed from a wound or to vomit. It is quite another thing to bathe in these things.

We need to recognize that, if we belong to Christ, then we have already died with Him, and cruelty and/or pain cannot affect the dead. Rather than this being a nice, theological concept, we need to ask the Lord to reveal this to us in our spirits by His Spirit and to make it real in our experience. Though pain is real, it need not be lasting and controlling. We must not keep harping on the injustices and the pains that we have had to endure.

He Who never did wrong in any way suffered unjustly and immeasurably, yet, He never gave in to self-pity because His focus was not on Himself but on His Father. He always sought to please His Father, not Himself. In so doing, He received strength from his Father that enabled Him to overcome every obstacle that came against His desire to fulfill His Father's will. Nothing deterred Him from His resolute purpose of living only to bring God joy and satisfaction. Now, the strength that was His is offered to us if we will turn our eyes totally on Him. Jesus Christ beckons to us to come to Him just as we are. If we will respond obediently to His call, open completely to Him, and be completely content with His will, He will be to us all that we need. Let's let Him comfort us, strengthen us, hold us, heal us, deliver us, empower us, and send us. Let us not give sinful hatred, bitterness, and unforgiveness any place in us. Instead, let us do good to those who wrong us, speak blessings on those who curse us, and embrace those who reject us. We will be able to do all of this by being so in love with Jesus that we keep our eyes on Him, not on our circumstances. Then, we shall find ourselves fulfilling His Royal Law of love, and He will bless us for it.

Practical Pointers On The Peaceful Path

We can begin a healing process within our innermost being by choosing to consider, reckon, and declare that the old part of us, the "us" apart from Christ, is dead. Also, we must not become caught-up in or overtaken with the things below—all that is of the physical, temporal realm. Instead, we must be certain to place and keep the focus of our hearts and minds on things above, in the spiritual realm, in Heaven and on Him Who sits on Heaven's throne. [Romans 6:11; Colossians 3:1-4; Hebrews 12:2]. We must look away from all that would distract—the good, the bad, and the ugly (all the "yuk") and, instead, look steadfastly at Jesus. [Hebrews 12:1-3.] He endured so many abuses and such incomparable, horrible pain, that Isaiah 53:3 referred to Him as a Man of sorrows who was acquainted with grief. In Luke 22:28, He even referred to His time of ministry as His trials. Yet, in John 15:11 and 17:13, he admitted He was joyful. He walked in a joy and a peace that went even deeper than pain. [John 14:27; 15:11; Hebrews 1:8-9].

He is still more than able to perfect that same unconquerable joy within us, regardless of the traumas of our past, present, or future. He has given to us His own peace and joy. Though we will have hard times in this present world, if we are focused on pleasing Jesus by living in obedience to Him, we will find ourselves becoming full of joy, courage, and confidence, for He *already has overcome* the world. [See John 14:27; 16:22-2; 17:13.]

Our joy, therefore, is not based on whether things are tough or easy, happy or sad. Instead, our joy stems from Jesus Christ Himself. The more we are captivated with Him and His interests, the more joy we will partake of, regardless of circumstances.

Just getting our eyes off of ourselves brings healing in and of itself, for we were not designed to be self-centered. Self-absorption is self-destructive. This is not to imply that we are not to care for ourselves. To the contrary, I am saying that the best thing we can ever do for ourselves is not to live with a self-centered mindset. When we live for the glory of God and the good of others instead of merely how to satisfy our own carnal lusts, ambitions, and petty selfishness, we place ourselves in the process of healing which leads to wholeness.

Joyful Even When We Are Not Happy

This doesn't mean that painful memories will make us feel good, but neither do they have to disturb our joy and peace. As we have previously touched on briefly in chapter fourteen, happiness is a surface emotion, more shallow than the character quality called "joy." Happiness is usually dependent on pleasant circumstances. Joy, on the other hand, runs deep. It is not affected by fluctuating circumstances because its source is in God Who never changes. It is a fruit of the Spirit—a character trait of Jesus Christ which is placed in us by His Spirit and which continues to develop in us as we abide in Christ by living in obedience to Him. Therefore, we can be full of joy and yet not feel happy. This is why Jesus Christ is referred to in Isaiah 53:3 as "...a Man of sorrows...aquainted with grief," and yet, at the same time, Psalm 45:7 and Hebrews 1:9 reveal that He was anointed with the oil of joy more than anyone else. He wasn't always happy, but He was joyful. Similarly, we can have the Holy Spirit's pure, inner waters of joy flowing deeply in our beings, even in the midst of unhappy times of sorrow, suffering, and grief.

However, like our Lord Jesus, if we are to walk in joy, we must love righteousness (and this infers that we *live* righteously). We cannot hold onto bitterness, wrath, rage, unforgiveness, and other carnal, destructive emotions and attitudes and expect to walk in the joy of the Lord. We must embrace the Savior and His example of wisdom, obedience, and love that He gave to us, trusting God to work all things out in the end.

To the degree that we are fretting, to that degree we are not letting the grace of God work fully in our lives and enable us to walk in righteousness. Therefore, we must see to it that we abide at rest in Christ Jesus and that our focus remains fixed on Him and His victorious, eternal kingdom, not this present world and its passing, pressing troubles.

Joy—The Reward Of Righteousness

Whenever we find ourselves "down in the dumps," we should examine our talk and our walk. Remember, according to Proverbs 18:20 and 21, "A man's moral self shall be filled with the fruit of his mouth, and with the consequence of his words he must be satisfied [whether good or evil]. Death and life are in the power of the tongue, and they who indulge it shall eat the fruit of it [for death or life]." And, as we have seen, if we do not live upright, holy lives, we shall not experience the joy of the Lord—we must walk the talk *and* talk the walk.

Let's not be too quick to blame a bad mood or "bummer vibe" on our diet, heredity, environment, "what Mama and/or Daddy did or did not do," moodiness, artistic and/or Irish/"I'm a redhead" temperament, "they laughed at me and made fun of me," or anything else.

Our Lord certainly dealt with rejection—He came from the lowly town of Nazareth (remember Nathanael's words recorded in John 1:46, after he heard that Jesus was from Nazareth: "Nazareth! Can anything good come out of Nazareth?"). To the Roman occupying army, He was just another one of the despised, eccentric, religious, conquered Jews. In John 7:5, we read of a time in His life when His brothers didn't believe in Him. In fact, Mark 3:21 reveals that His family believed that He was "out of His mind." Apparently, even His mother Mary believed this at that time, for in verse thirty-one we find her with His brothers when they came "to take charge of Him." Remember what we have already considered in chapter fourteen concerning I Isaiah 53:3. We discovered that our Lord "was despised, rejected, and forsaken by men, a Man of sorrows and pains Who was acquainted with grief." We have also seen that in Luke 22:29, Jesus Himself referred to the period of time in which He ministered as His "trials."

No wonder Hebrews 5:7 says that during His earthly life, Jesus offered up prayers and petitions with loud cries and tears to God. And we know how, at the end of His earthly ministry, everyone forsook Him. Wow!!! Talk about what modern psychology would refer to as a textbook case of circumstances that would probably produce paranoia, deep-seated resentment, anger, depression, and extreme antisocial behavior. If anybody had an excuse for these or other personal problems, emotional scars, and aberrations, it was Jesus Christ. In the light of what He had to face, our problems and rejections seem petty.

This may not remove the pain of trials and rejection, but, if we will allow it, we can receive encouragement for our lives as we consider the difficulties He encountered and triumphantly overcame. Thus, we read in Hebrews 12:2 and 3, "Let us fix our eyes on Jesus, the Author and the Perfecter of our faith, Who for the joy set before him endured the cross, scorning and ignoring its shame, and sat down at the right hand of the throne of God, Consider Him Who endured such opposition and bitter hostility from sinners—consider it all in comparison with your trials—so that you may not grow weary or exhausted, losing heart and relaxing and fainting in your minds."

In spite of all He endured, our Lord was "together." He had no abnormal, emotional quirks, no sociopathic or psychopathic tendencies. To the contrary, He was full of genuine concern and love for others and was totally selfless, always thinking of others' welfare ahead of His own. Rather than being a sullen, morose, introspective, insecure person, He was outgoing, loving, giving...even joyful.

Hebrews 1:9 reveals the secret to His joy: Because our Lord Jesus loved righteousness and hated sin, He was anointed with the oil of joy and gladness beyond His companions. From this, we can deduce that if we will love righteousness and hate sin, we shall, like Him, be anointed mightily with the oil of joy and gladness. Consider also Matthew 5:6, where our Lord says that if we hunger and thirst for righteousness, we shall be filled. As we take all of these things together, we can conclude that righteousness is a product of our spiritual hunger and thirst for it, and joy is a by-product of righteousness. Therefore, we are not to seek joy, but righteousness, which, in turn will open the door to an anointing of joy.

Also, James 3:2 tells us that whoever can control his tongue is a mature person, able to control his whole body. In such a consecrated, set apart vessel, the Holy Spirit is pleased to manifest the joy, the presence, the purity, the power—yes, the very Person—of the Lord Jesus Christ.

The Judgment—The Great Equalizer/ Maintain The Eternal Perspective (E.P.)

Many (if not most) of the inequities, abuses, and acts of unfairness that we have faced begin to make sense only in the light of eternity and The Judgment. At The Judgment, God will see to it that those who have wrongfully suffered will be more than adequately repaid. So wonderful will be His mercies and so great His rewards for those who suffered injustices in this life that we probably will wish we had suffered more and gone through even greater maltreatment. To some degree, the amount of glory that we will partake of in eternity will correspond to the amount of darkness and hardship that we had to endure in this temporal realm.

Paul says in Romans 8:17 and 18, "...we must share Christ's sufferings if we are to share His glory. But what of that? For I consider that the sufferings of this present time (this present life) are not worth being compared with the glory that is about to be revealed to us and in us and for us, and conferred on us!" Furthermore, in 2 Corinthians 4:16-17, Paul writes, "...we do not become discouraged—utterly spiritless, exhausted, and wearied out through fear. Though outwardly we are decaying and wasting away, yet inwardly we are being renewed day by day. For our light and momentary affliction (this slight distress of the passing hour) is ever more and more abundantly preparing and producing and achieving for us an eternal weight of glory that far outweighs them all—beyond all measure, excessively surpassing all comparisons and all calculations, a vast and transcendent glory and blessedness never to cease!"

Then, Paul reveals that we are to look ahead to the coming glorious rewards for faithfulness to the Lord if we are to endure the present difficulties. Notice verse 18. After discussing present troubles and future rewards, Paul says, "Since we consider and look not to the things that are seen but to the things that are unseen; for the things that are visible are temporary, but what is unseen is eternal." Maintaining an eternal perspective in the midst of this fading, temporal world order will strengthen us and enable us to endure the difficulties of this present life. In the coming manifestation of God's Kingdom, all present sorrows and sighing will be forever removed, and we will endlessly enjoy being with the Lord and with those who are His.

Complete In Him

Apart from Christ, we're all a mess in some form or fashion. We've all been devastated and destroyed by the ravages of sin. However, those who are in Christ have been made complete and whole in Him. Colossians 2:9-10 says: "For in Him dwells all the fullness of the Godhead bodily; and you are complete in Him, who is the Head of all principality and power."

For those of us who know the Lord Jesus, we will walk in the reality of these verses if we choose to aggressively and tenaciously seek Him and lay hold of Him and all that He is in us. This is active, living faith that changes us completely. It's not always easy. In fact, sometimes it's tough—*real* tough. Just plain *hard.* But the rewards of character in this life and glory in the one yet to be revealed, make it all worthwhile. May we always remember that the darker the night, the greater the light; the greater the temporary pain, the greater the eternal gain; the greater the weight of burdens and even unjust sufferings we bear up under now, the greater the "weight of glory" will be on us then. Similarly, the more obedient we are to *wait on* the Lord, the more expedient will be our ability to bear a *weight* of glory *from* the Lord.

So, let's take heart and never give up. We will be strengthened and encouraged as we realize that the reality of experiencing the Lord God in a deeper, richer way is just beyond the cloud of darkness.

The "Light" Of Lucifer, Or The "Darkness" Of The Lord?

May we not be deceived by Lucifer—the one whose name means "light-bringer" or "shining one." Though he is the prince of darkness in whom there is no light, he masquerades as an angel of light. Surrounding himself with a semblance of light with which he was once filled, and offering a false "peace" (so-called), he leads his followers into dense darkness, total devastation, and utter ruin.

Instead, let us follow the call of the Lord and forever embrace Him Who—though surrounding Himself with thick darkness, devouring fire, and a raging tempest—dwells in unimaginable light, healing balm, and comforting calm to all who are proven faithful to Him...

If we will press doggedly through the darkness by His grace,
we will find God (in Whom there is no darkness)
waiting for us, desirous for fellowship and union with us.

If we will face and enter into the devouring fire,
we will find that our God has devoured the bondages
that have held us back and tied us down
from growing and soaring in Him.

And if we will not falter and forsake the Lord
when facing raging tempests,
we will find Him to be ever faithful and true,
the One Who is able to calm the troubled seas with His word.
Forever He shall be the only One Who can bring perfect calm
to situations that, only a moment before,
were turbulent, threatening, and terrifying.

And, if we have ears to hear,
we should rejoice in the knowledge that we already sit with
Christ in God in heavenly places.
There is *nothing* that can separate us from the love of God
in Jesus the Messiah—His Son and our loving Savior.

Therefore, we need not fear God rejecting us,
for, through Jesus, we have been brought *forever* near.

In Jesus' mighty, healing arms of perfect peace and liberating love and light, we will find ourselves enveloped, comforted, and transformed. By His Holy Spirit, we shall be partakers of the total, inner transformations that occur in all who are blessed to experience the tests, trials, tribulations, and ultimate triumph of the mind-renewing, heart-transforming reality of *"God's Psychology."*

NOTE: For further discussion regarding light and darkness and their roles in the plan of God, see chapter 10: "The Treasures Of Darkness" located in *The Passionate Pursuit—Living In Love With Jesus Christ*, Volume 3 of "The Highest Calling Of All" Series by Larry Trammell.

Closing Thoughts

Within the preceding pages, the Spirit of God has called to us to give ourselves completely to Jesus, looking to Him as our only source of hope, deliverance, and complete salvation. God loved the world so much that He gave His Son to pay the price to buy us back from the "slave block" of selfishness, sin, and death.

Now it's our move.

When we hear His voice, we must not harden our hearts. Instead, we must call out to Him, turning to Him and believing on Him—clinging to Him as our only hope of deliverance and salvation. It is only by coming to Him, needingly and receptively, that we can ever please God and be at peace with Him and ourselves.

If we first establish relationship with Him, we will be one of those trees of righteousness of which Isaiah 61:1-3 speaks. As Paul wrote in Colossians 2:6-7, we are to let our roots go down deeply into Jesus Christ. If we will abide in Him through obedience to Him by His mercy and grace, the waters of God's life will flow like a river in us, quenching all of our spiritual thirst and enabling us to bear the fruit of the Holy Spirit—the very character qualities of Christ.

We are called to eternally enjoy wonderful, intimate, loving fellowship and relationship with Him beyond what we can even imagine. Let's not be deceived by the erroneous thought that genuine fellowship with God can be had without first establishing a relationship with Him as one of His very own, spiritually "reborn" people.

The Challenging, Joyful, Never Ending Journey

As we come to the end of this book, I pray that it will help you get on with your journey—the journey of the perception and pursuit of God and His will. Thank God, it is a journey of love from God and for God, full of devotion to Him through His Son and the power of His Holy Spirit. Nevertheless, it is difficult, fraught with much pain from selfishness, Satan, and sin, and filled with many obstacles placed in our path by a murderous enemy. However, it is also the most joyful, fulfilling, and purposeful of journeys that ultimately leads to the most gain, for it leads us straight into the Heavenly Father's arms. Only as we apply all of our energies to completing this journey will we experience the real reason for which we were created—to know God, love God, and obey God in a never-ending, ever-deepening relationship with Him and His Son. Furthermore, this journey of journeys shall last forever—endlessly, it will take us deeper and deeper into the very depths and nature of the heart, mind, and soul of Jesus Christ—He Whom we pursue diligently and adore exceedingly more than all else.

If you have not yet begun this most important and awesome of journeys into the very heart of God and of His kingdom, then I strongly urge you to begin *now.* Call out to God for salvation. It is the first step to becoming saved from sin, Satan, and self. Declare to Jesus your need of Him. Accept the fact that He took the punishment we all deserve for our rebellion against God and is the only door to the Heavenly Father. Give yourself to Him. Open your heart by an act of your will and receive Jesus Christ as your Lord and Savior. If you do so, He will give you the gift of eternal, spiritual life and begin an inner work of transformation in you that will cause your character to become more and more like Him.

Come home—home to the arms and love of your Creator. He is waiting for you.

As you embark and travel down the road of life on this journey, do not be amazed when others mock you.

You have left "Broad Street" and are traveling a far less frequented, narrow avenue called 'the Highway of Holiness."

Although many will think you are crazy for leaving the road more frequently traveled, it really doesn't matter what anybody else thinks. You have heard Him call, and His call is for you to travel on the road He has placed you. Yes, it is far less traveled, but those who have gone before have left us clear markers of encouragement and refreshments to give us strength.

Help others along the way, whether that means showing the way to get onto the Highway of Holiness or if they just need encouragement not to quit on their journey. As you give to others, you will receive, and as you minister to them, you will receive ministry. If you know that you are needy, then give, and what you truly need will be given to you. This is a principle of the kingdom on whose road you now travel.

Read the Scriptures and other books that will direct your gaze on Him who is your Goal and Destination. Do not allow yourself to be distracted by things off the well-worn, proven Path Of Eternal Perception And Pursuit—the path called "Faith." The Lord is with you, saying, "This is the way—walk in it."

Know that He will tell you the way to go, but you must obey Him or you will get nowhere. "You cannot steer a parked car." So, get on with the will of God for you. Do not be deceived into thinking that merely studying a map (such as the Bible or another book like this particular one) is the same as reaching your destination. Only obedience to the Lord will get you there.

Ask Him to fill you with His Holy Spirit. It is only by the power of His Spirit that you will be equipped with all that you need to live a victorious life over the world, the flesh, and the devil. Tell the Lord that you want everything that He has provided for you so that you can become and do all that He desires.

Don't be discouraged as you encounter difficulties on your journey, including various lusts and contrariness that arise from within you. Always remember this important fact: God knows all of your weaknesses and evil tendencies, yet loves you unconditionally and accepts you fully in Jesus Christ His Son—He Who is your righteousness.

Dear saint, know that you are loved...
You are adored...
You are accepted in Jesus—
there is nothing you could ever do
that would cause God to love you more.
You are known—
God speaks your name with tears of joy in His eyes
and sings over you with joy.
He is always thinking about you and is always with you—
you are *never* alone...
And know that He loves to hear your voice calling His name
and speaking words of love and holy desire for Him.

He knows what you face and endure. Your struggles are not unique. Others have dealt with the same kind of things you have faced, are now facing, or even yet will face. Do not be disheartened, neither think that He is surprised at what you are capable of thinking or doing. He knows of what you are made, and for this reason, He is using the journey to prepare you for your eternal destination of living forever in His very presence, fellowshipping with Him in an ongoing, ever-deepening relationship.

Know that your life is not primarily on display on this journey as an artifact to be gawked at or even fully admired by God or by others. Rather, it is a journey fraught with trials and the exposing of self in all of its ugliness so that you can yield more aggressively to the Lord, laying hold of His mercy and grace to overcome the tendencies of your mind and its "earthsuit."

So, don't become frustrated with others or yourself as you continue in "the way of truth and of the Lord." Instead, be encouraged, knowing that "He who began a good work in you will complete it..."—just as we read in Philippians 1:6. Having begun The Journey, never quit...

> *Having turned from sin, don't go back again.*
> *But if you do, then do this, too:*
> *Run to Jesus—the One Who frees us.*
> *Repent and confess and re-enter God's rest.*

Do not allow yourself to become depressed or even disappointed and angry with God because of difficulties you shall encounter (and you certainly shall encounter them). Remember that, often, God is more interested in getting a problem out of us rather than in getting us out of a problem.

Also, as we shall study in much more detail in THE PASSIONATE PURSUIT—Living In Love With Jesus Christ (the next book in "The Highest Calling Of All" series), Jesus did not come to bless you. Instead, He came to *kill* you. That is, He desires to end your life of self-centeredness (you are to offer it up willingly to Him), replacing it with His resurrection life as you are centered on Him. He desires that you allow Him to make Himself at home in you as your very life. [Remember, He wants a habitation, not just a visitation.] He came to bring you to the end of your ways so that you could truly know His ways, for the end of our ways mark the beginning of His.

Turn from sin to the joy of obeying the Spirit of the Living God. He is your Guide on the journey, and He will see you through to the end as long as you do not turn away from Him by spurning and rejecting His dealings. Jesus has promised *never* to forsake you. By relying on and drawing strength from His grace, do not forsake Him.

Let nothing cause a disturbance of your confidence in Him and of the intimate union and fellowship to which He calls you to enjoy with Him. Therefore, if you sin, be quick to turn back to Him in repentance and confession of your sins to Him. Next, be quick to forgive yourself, get up, and keep on keepin' on...

So, even if you stumble, don't stop. Get up, brush yourself off, and get on with the journey.

They Journey On The Journey

Be kind and understanding to everyone, particularly they who travel on the same path as the one on which you trod to your Heavenly Home in the arms of your Heavenly Father. They journey on The Journey with you—they are your fellow sojourners—and are subject to the same weariness, tests, and temptations that you face.

We are all so weak and needy of Jesus and of one another, and we shall receive of God's mercy according to the amount of mercy we extend to others. Therefore, remember your frailties and need of the Lord, and this in turn will help you to have patience and understanding to others who are also needy.

He Who alone is the King and Judge is Faithful and True, and He is in love with you. Quickly now, therefore, without delay, forsake the things of this present, soon-to-disappear-forever world and press on to your Father's arms and the tender embrace of His Son.

Consider the power and greatness of God's gift for those who were once His enemies: When we were sinners, separated from God because of our stubborn rebellion against Him and His authority, He willed the death of His Son to secure our release from sin and its just condemnation. Now consider how much greater is the unrestricted power and greatness of Christ's resurrection life that is available to those of us who choose to respond to His call to become totally His. We read of these wonderful things in Romans 5:10: "...if while we were enemies [of God] we were reconciled [to Him] through the death of His Son, it is much more certain, now that we are reconciled, that we shall be saved [daily delivered from sin's dominion] through His resurrection life." He offers us the blessing of His resurrection life in exchange for the curse of eternal death that was upon us—thank God!

Always remember: The Journey begins and ends with Jesus. As He Himself said in The Revelation 21:6,

"I Am

the A and the Z;

the beginning and the end."

"As you have therefore received Christ Jesus as Lord, continue to live in *Him*—in union with *Him* and in conformity to *Him*. Have the roots of your being firmly and deeply planted in *Him*—fixed and founded in *Him*—being continually built up in *Him*, becoming increasingly more confirmed and established in the faith, just as you were taught, and abounding and overflowing in it with thanksgiving."
[Colossians 2:6-7]

Yes, let's be in love with Jesus and in pursuit of Him—The Quest.

As we begin and look to complete *The Journey*, always remember to keep in mind the One by Whom we live and for Whom we belong—Jesus Christ—The Journey's Beginning, Destination, and End.

Read the following words and meditate on them. Allow God's thoughts entrance into your heart. By His Spirit, daily walk in His light. His words are signposts on the narrow pathway of life and will equip you to be able to steer clear of the broad highway of death...

Read And Take Heed!

"If anyone would come after Me, he must deny himself—
that is, disown himself, forget, lose sight of himself
and his own interests, refuse and give up himself—
and take up His cross daily,
and follow Me (cleaving steadfastly to Me).
For whoever would preserve and wants to save his life
will lose it, but whoever loses his life for My sake will save it."
Yeshua HaMashiach (Jesus The Messiah); Luke 9:23-24

"...[I] say...with tears, many live as enemies of the cross of Christ.
Their destiny is destruction, their god is their stomach,
and their glory is in their shame. Their mind is on earthly things.
But our citizenship is in Heaven (it is our homeland).
And we eagerly await a Savior from there, the Lord Jesus Christ..."
Philippians 3:18-20

Since, then, you have been raised with Christ,
set your hearts on things above, where Christ is,
seated at the right hand of God.
And set your minds and keep them set on what is above,
not on earthly things.
Colossians 3:1-2

[To an unbelieving ruler named Felix,
the apostle Paul shared the gospel, discoursing on]...
righteousness,
self-control,
and the Judgment to come.
Acts 24:25

"You diligently study the Scriptures because you *think*
that by them you have eternal life.
These are the Scriptures that testify about *Me,*
yet you refuse to come to Me so that you might have life."
**Jesus Christ—The Way, the Truth, the Life (John 14:6),
and the only Savior; John 5:39-40**

[Some people asked Jesus] "...What are we to do to carry out
what God requires?" Jesus replied, "This is the work (the
service) that God asks of you, that you *cleave to Me."*
John 6:28-29

Let our people also learn to maintain good works,
to meet urgent needs, that they might not be unfruitful.
Titus 3:14

Carry each other's burdens,
and in this way you will fulfill the law of Christ.
Galatians 6:2

"The person who has My commands and *obeys* them
is the one who loves Me, and whoever loves Me will be loved
by My Father. And I too will love that person
and will *show (reveal, manifest) Myself* to him—
I will let Myself be *clearly seen* by him
and *make Myself real* to him."
**Jesus Christ—The Mystic Secret of God (Colossians 2:2);
John 14:21**

We know that we have come to know Him
if we obey His commands.
1 John 2:4

"...if you have not been trustworthy in handling
the unrighteous mammon—worldly wealth, possessions—
who will entrust to you the true riches?
**Jesus—The Giver of the true riches:
Him and His kingdom; Luke 16:11**

"Not everyone who says to Me, 'Lord, Lord,' will enter into
the kingdom of Heaven, but only those who do the will of
My Father Who is in Heaven. Many will say to Me on that Day,
'Lord, Lord, did we not prophesy in Your name,
and in Your name cast out demons,
and in Your name perform many miracles?'
Then I will tell them plainly, 'I never knew you. Depart from Me,
you who practice lawlessness—disregarding My commands!' "
**Jesus Christ—The King of God's eternal kingdom
Matthew 7:21-23**

"...the ones sown among the thorns are others who hear the Word,
then the cares and anxieties of the world—the worries of this life,
and distractions of the age, and the pleasure and delight and
false glamour and deceitfulness of riches, and the craving and
passionate desire (the lust) for other things
creep in and choke the Word, and it becomes unfruitful."
**The Lord Jesus—The Sower Who has sown His Word
in our hearts; Mark 4:18-19**

"...that which is exalted and highly thought of, esteemed and
valued among men is detestable and abhorrent
and an abomination in the sight of God."
**Jesus—The One Who knows what God the Father
hates and loves; Luke 16:15b**

...[Moses] never flinched but held staunchly to his purpose
and endured steadfastly as one who gazed on Him Who is invisible.
Hebrews 11:27b

"Anyone who receives a prophet because he is a prophet
shall receive a prophet's reward,
and anyone who receives a righteous man
because he is a righteous man will receive a righteous man's reward.
And if anyone gives even a cup of cold water to one of these
little ones because he is My disciple, I tell you the truth,
he will certainly not lose his reward."
**The Lord Jesus—The Rewarder & ultimate Reward
Matthew 10:41-42**

"I am the True Vine and My Father is the Vinedresser.
Any branch in Me that does not bear fruit—that stops bearing—
He cuts away (trims off, takes away).
And He cleanses and repeatedly prunes every branch
that continues to bear fruit, to make it bear
more and richer and more excellent fruit...
I am the Vine, you are the branches.
Whoever lives in Me and I in him bears much fruit.
However, apart from Me—cut off from vital union with Me—
you can do *nothing*.

Jesus Christ—The Vine; John 15:1 & 5

If then you have been raised up with Christ,
set your hearts on things above,
where Christ is seated at the right hand of God.
And set your minds and keep them set on what is above—
the higher things—not on the things that are on the earth.
You should have as little desire for this world as a dead person
does. Your real life is in Heaven with Christ in God.

Colossians 3:1-3

My dear children, I write this to you so that you will not sin.
But if anybody does sin, we have one who speaks to the Father
in our defense—Jesus Christ, the Righteous One.

1 John 2:1

...[Believers,] count yourselves dead to sin
but alive to God in Christ Jesus.

Romans 6:11

...one thing I do—it is my one aspiration: forgetting what lies behind
and straining forward to what lies ahead, I press on toward the goal
to win the [supreme and heavenly] prize
to which God in Christ Jesus is calling us upward.

Paul, the apostle; Philippians 3:13b-14

The sins of some people are obvious, going ahead of them
to the judgment seat and proclaiming their sentence in advance;
but the sins of others appear later—following the offender to the
bar of judgment and coming into view there.
In the same way, good deeds are obvious,
and even when they are not, they cannot remain hidden.
1 Timothy 5:24-25

I am not conscious of anything against myself, and I feel blameless;
but I am not vindicated and acquitted before God on that account.
It is the Lord Himself Who examines and judges me.
So do not make any hasty or premature judgments
before the time when the Lord comes again,
for He will both bring to light the secret things
that are now hidden in darkness,
and disclose and expose the secret aims
(the motives and purposes) of hearts.
Then every man will receive his due commendation from God.
Paul; 1 Corinthians 4:4-5

Make every effort to live in peace with all men and to be holy;
without holiness no one will see the Lord.
Hebrews 12:14

God will give to each person according to what he has done.
To those who by persistence in doing good
seek glory, honor, and immortality, He will give eternal life.
But for those who are self-seeking and who reject the truth
and follow evil, there will be wrath and anger...
God by Jesus Christ will judge everyone
in regard to the things which they conceal—
their hidden thoughts and secrets...
Romans 2:7, 8, & 16b

The one who says, "I know Him,"
but does not do what He commands is a liar,
and the truth is not in that person.
1 John 2:4

"Behold, I am coming soon,
and I shall bring My wages and rewards with Me,
to repay and render to each one according to what he has *done*."
**Jesus Christ—The Lord of Glory and Judge of all
The Revelation Of Jesus Christ 22:12**

The conclusion, when all has been heard, is:
Fear God and obey His commandments,
for this is the whole duty of man.
For God shall bring every deed into judgment,
including every hidden thing, whether good or evil.
Ecclesiastes 12:13-14

Blessed are those who wash their robes,
that they may have the right to the tree of life and may
go through the gates into the city. Outside are the dogs,
those who practice magic arts, the sexually immoral,
the murderers, the idolaters,
and everyone who loves and practices lying.
The Revelation 22:14-15

Wonder Of Wonders

(a song)

Wonder of wonders—Christ within.
Wonder of wonders—to be freed from all sin.
From glory to glory and faith to faith,
we're growing in Jesus by His grace.

Learning to trust Him, yes, we're learning to yield.
We're learning to move only in His perfect will.
We're growing in wisdom and in the love of God.
Abiding in Jesus, we are cleansed by His blood.

**(chorus) Wonder of wonders is the Lord Jesus Christ—
God's mystic secret—our very life. He reveals Himself to,
then within, then through those who answer His call.
Yes, the Wonder of wonders is Jesus—the Lord of all!**

Resting in Jesus, for He is our life.
We are the branches, and He is the Vine.
We're gazing unto Him as we run the race.
We're changed into His image, beholding His face.

**(chorus) Wonder of wonders is the Lord Jesus Christ—
God's mystic secret—our very life. He reveals Himself to,
then within, then through those who answer His call.
Yes, the Wonder of wonders is Jesus—the Lord of all!**

Larry Trammell/ Ablaze Publishing/ (770) 476-0230/ © 8/1982

The Journey

There's a journey that's before us
and a race that's to be won.
And only those who start will win
through Jesus Christ, God's Son.

Fast comes an enemy to us
to keep us from our Goal.
But if we'll lean hard on God
we may rock, but we won't roll.

Tomorrow may be too late
so don't wait to cast away
the things of earth and flesh—
prepare today for Judgment Day!

This journey of all journey's
on a straight and narrow road,
so qualify to be
the Father's and the Son's abode.

This will happen as you listen and obey
Christ's holy word,
so be sure to be a doer
of His Truth that You have heard.

Cling to Jesus always—
'tis the way of victory.
And, all who overcome,
will walk with Him eternally.

So, let's head on toward God's city
without selfish pride and sin.
On That Day, may He say to us,
"stay with Me—The Journey's End."

Larry Trammell/ Ablaze Publishing/ (770) 476-0230/ © 3/17/2001

*D*id the Spirit of the Lord speak to you through the contents of this book? If so, please consider before God whether He would be pleased for you to donate to this ministry, perhaps with a one-time gift or on an ongoing basis. When we give blessing in return for blessing, this is honorable to the Lord Jesus. Also, know that your giving will help to propagate His message in these pages to others.

Please, whether or not you give monetarily, earnestly pray for us that we will fully please Jesus without compromise.

Also, contact us if you desire to have Larry and/or others with Ablaze Ministries to visit and assist you in magnifying the Lord Jesus the Messiah and declaring His matchless word.

Ablaze Ministries   P.O. Box 956236
Duluth, GA   USA   30095-9504
770.476.0230, ext. 2   Fax: 770.622.3064

E-Mail & Internet Website:
www.ablazeministries.com

Ablaze Ministries' Materials
Books/Booklets From "The Highest Calling Of All" Series

Volume 1: The Highest Calling Of All—God's Ultimate Purpose For Each Of Us [ISBN 0-9624370-0-X] touches on many topics ranging from repentance and salvation to deep relationship with God and His people. Being a template of sorts for the remainder of the series, its contents are actually contained and more thoroughly expounded in the following books and tapes:

Volume 2: The Journey—God's Call & Provision For Us To Begin & Complete Our Return To Him [ISBN 0-9624370-2-6] calls sinners to God through Jesus Christ and gives instructions to His disciples who are facing obstacles on their spiritual journey.

Volume 3: The Passionate Pursuit—Living In Love With Jesus Christ [ISBN 0-9624370-3-4] is a book concerning the love and longing of Christ for a bride who is in love with *Him*, not merely His blessings, position, and power.

Volume 4: Romantic Relationship With God, Not Ritualistic Religion About God—Substitutes Leave Us Destitute [ISBN 0-9624370-4-2] calls us to forsake the religious thinking of humanity and to truly lay hold of the Lord Himself.

Volume 5: Let God Arise In His People—He Wants To Speak *To* His People, *Through* His People [ISBN 0-9624370-5-0] challenges *every* saint to become a minister of the New Covenant. Servant-leaders are raised up to stir up (not beat up) the saints. They are to serve and motivate as wise and loving parents, coaches, or ushers, not dominate in a "one-man-show." The book encourages us individually and corporately to become an instrument of expression for the Son of God—a living, relationship-with-God-and-one-another-based organism, not a dead, ritual-and-rules-laden-based organization.

Volume 6: Romancing The Throne—A Lifestyle Of Praise & Worship Born In Heaven [ISBN 0-9624370-1-8] Although containing some practical, "how to" instructions, it focuses even more on inspiring and inflaming hearts—wooing them—to be in love with the Lord and to woo Him, producing lifestyles marked by praise and worship, instant and consistent obedience, holiness, zeal, and love. The book goes hand in hand with the music CD/tape: *"Enter-In..."*

Volume 7: Genuine FAITH—The Eternal Perspective: Perceiving And Pursuing God And His Eternal, Invisible Kingdom [ISBN 0-9624370-7-7] reveals the essence of true, biblical faith. Saints are to be temporary sojourners "just passing through" this visible, temporary realm who have their hearts firmly set on perceiving and pursuing the unseen, eternal realm of the Kingdom of God. The contents show that real discipleship to Jesus Christ is not centered on how to persuade God to cater to our desires and do our will, but on His requirement that we forsake our own ways and all other loves to live totally in love with Him and *His* will.

Volume 8: Walk The Talk—Loving God Means Obeying God [ISBN 0-9624370-8-5] discusses the necessity of practicing what we preach and to walk in love with others as well as with God. It calls us to deeply love the Lord and one another and to experience the transformation of our hearts, not just accrue information in our minds. Much "how to" instruction is included.

Volume 9: Prepare The Way Of The Lord!!! *A Prophetic Call & Warning For Each Of Us* [ISBN 0-9624370-9-3] contains a wake-up call for repentance and a message of wooing and warning from the Spirit of God with the intention of leading those who have ears to hear to a close(r) relationship and fellowship with the Living God. This book challenges us to count the cost and pay the price to live in God's glory through our love for and obedience to Him, thereby hastening the Lord Jesus' return.

Volume 10: **The 1ˢᵗ Poetic Prophetic**—*Poetic Prophecies, Psalms, & Prayers* [ISBN 0-9624370-6-9] is the first volume of what will probably become an ongoing collection. Having over one hundred entries, the book is profound, prophetic, and powerful, particularly when accompanied by the audio recording of Larry reading it. Reprints of the individual titles are available, suitable for framing, on a per request basis.

Volumes 11-14: *Treasures Of Truth*—Words Of Wisdom & Practical Instruction To Help Overcomers Overcome [Volume 11: ISBN 0-9714637-1-9; Volume 12: ISBN 0-9714637-2-7; Volume 13: ISBN 0-9714637-3-5; Volume 14: ISBN 0-9714637-4-3] is a series in and of itself, currently consisting of a set of seven compilations contained in four different books. They read very much like the book of Proverbs and will prove to be tremendous helps for personal meditations and group discussions. Speakers and teachers will find them to be ready and superb sources for timely topics as well as for "power phrases" that will add thought provoking impact to presentations.

NOTE: Volumes 1 through 9 have workbooks available that are beneficial for individual and/or group study. *Also,* check with Ablaze Ministries concerning potential college credit for satisfactorily completing *"The Highest Calling Of All" Series* correspondence course.

The Highest Calling Of All" Series is not only available in print [entire printed series: ISBN 0-9624370-0-0], *but also in recorded formats (read by Larry).*
Printed/recorded packages may be purchased at a discount if bought together.

ALSO AVAILABLE:

(1) Music and teaching CDs and tapes that will bless you. In particular, a 3 CD/ Tape set that is full of spontaneity and life of Alice and Larry worshiping the Lord, entitled *"Enter In—Times of Intimacy With Our Lord, Savior, And Promised Husband—Jesus Christ."* The CDs are appropriately entitled: "The Outer Court;" "The Holy Place;" & "The Holy Of Holies." This recording has touched many people very deeply. It is simple and sweet, yet often speaks deeply to and challenges the heart. The set contains some songs that Larry has written, as well as spontaneous songs ("new songs") and prayers to the Lord, along with prophetic, musical responses from the Lord. Prophetic teachings it contains urge and assist seeking listeners to enter in and worship the Lord and to make their callings and elections certain and steadfast. Also, a single CD consisting of selections from the three CD set is available, entitled "Sampler."

(2) Tote bags ("You're a Dream of God Come True!").

(3) "Truth Threads" that include **T-Shirts** (*"T's of Truth,"* including: "The Caboose Is Loose—Makin' New Tracks, Not Lookin' Back"; "No More Stinkin' Thinkin'—Dreams At Work; "JESUS IS THE WAY," and many others that are planned) and **Sweats** ("Overcomer!").

—Quantity Discounts Are Available—
See your favorite Christian materials supplier, or contact us at:

Ablaze Ministries P.O. Box 956236 Duluth, GA USA 30095-9504
Office: 770.476.0230   Fax: 770.622.3064
E-Mail and Internet Website: www.ablazeministries.com

The Trammells
—Alice, Larry, Stacy, & Cliff—
(December 2002)

About The Author & Much Of His Message

"To help prepare a bride for the Son of God—a people who care for one another and are totally, deeply, and very passionately in love with Jesus Christ" is what Larry Trammell has said regarding the reason he was born. To that end, since 1971, through prophetic worship, teaching, preaching, books, and music, Larry has proclaimed a call to cling to the Lord Himself and not just things *about* Him, as well as the Lord's command to love one another, by His grace.

"In 1 Corinthians 14, we see that the gatherings of the saints are to be times of ministry to the Lord and from the Lord through *all* of those gathered," says Larry. "As we love on God—worshiping Him with **all** of our hearts, souls, minds, and strength—He ministers back to us all and through us all, if we will but allow Him to do so. Let us not limit Him through our unbelief and clinging to the traditions of men. Instead, may we ever 'let God arise' (just as Psalm 68:1 says) by allowing the Son of God to have full expression through *every* member of His body. We need to hear what God is saying *to* His people, *through* His people—*all* of them—not merely 'through a certain few while all the rest watch but don't do.' Certainly, there are leaders in the church, just as Ephesians 4, 1 Peter 5, Hebrews 13 and other Scriptures tell us, but they are to be *servant-leaders* whose aim is to equip their brothers and sisters in Christ to do the work of the ministry—first to the Lord, then to others. Much of this equipping work involves their drawing out of the saints what God has already placed in His people.

"The secret of victory in Christ is to maintain the eternal perspective of genuine faith—ever perceiving and pursuing the eternal, unseen things above of Christ and His kingdom—instead of being caught up with things below: the cares of this life, the deceitfulness of riches, and the lust for other things—all of which shall soon be gone forever. No matter what it costs us—and He does require that we forsake *all* of *our* concepts, dreams, plans, passions, purposes, pursuits…and, yes, even *our very lives—Jesus is worth it all.* Only by forsaking everything else can we know Him most intimately, and we will realize ultimate fulfillment as we live to bring joy and delight to His heart. May we never cease to "enter in" to sincere, Spirit-led praise and worship to the true and living God—our Abba; our Papa. Why? Simply *because He likes it.* Only as we die to self can we live to God and hear Him say to us on That Day, 'Well done, good and faithful servant! *Enter in…*' "

In 1994, Larry and his family began pastoring a flock that first began gathering in their house near Atlanta, Georgia (USA), and are available, as the Lord wills, to share the deposits God has worked and placed in them. These include: an emphasis on maintaining eternal perspective—"E.P." (with its accompanying eternal focus and pursuit); relationship with Jesus over religious forms; proclaiming God's highest calling of intimacy with a holy people who love one another and who love Him more than His blessings; sharing how to "walk the talk" in our daily lives and routines; instruction regarding having genuine and honest relationships with the Lord and with one another that grow ever-deeper; leading others into Holy Spirit-led, spontaneous and non-platform-focused ministry to and from the Lord in praise and worship; prophesying, preaching, and teaching in word, song, dance, and drama; and conducting marriage/family life seminars.

Your prayers for the Trammells are *greatly* appreciated.

They may be reached and/or you can be placed on their mailing list by contacting them:

Ablaze Ministries   Box 956236
Duluth, GA (USA)   30095-9504   770.476.0230
E-Mail and Internet Website: www.ablazeministries.com

Printed in the United States
1152500005B/199